ONE WOMAN

Against REICH
the

The True Story of a Mother's Struggle to Keep Her
Family Faithful to God in a World Gone Mad

HELMUT W. ZIEFLE

Kregel
Publications

One Woman Against the Reich

© 2003 by Helmut W. Ziefle

Published by Kregel Publications, a division of Kregel, Inc., P.O. Box 2607, Grand Rapids, MI 49501.

Translated by permission from the German edition *Gegen Hitler und das Reich,* © 2000 by Helmut Ziefle. Published by Ernst Franz & Sternberg Verlag, Riederich (Metzingen).

The names of certain individuals have been abbreviated in the interest of privacy. Also, casual acquaintances have been given assumed names due to the long time that has elapsed since the encounters.

Library of Congress Cataloging-in-Publication Data
Ziefle, Helmut W.
[Gegen Hitler und das Reich, English]
One woman against the Reich / by Helmut W. Ziefle.
    p. cm.
"…revised and expanded version"—Pref.
    1. Ziefle, Maria. 2. Ziefle family. 3. Anti-Nazi movement—Germany—Heilbronn. 4. Sontheim (Heilbronn, Germany)—Biography. 5. Heilbronn (Germany)—Biography. 6. Christian biography—Germany—Heilbronn. I. Title.
DD901.S654 Z53813   2003
943'.47—dc21   2002152257

ISBN 0-8254-4159-5

Printed in the United States of America

05 06 07 08 09 / 6 5 4 3 2

ONE WOMAN

Against the REICH

Maria Ziefle, wife and mother of four—a Christian role model in difficult times.

To my parents,
who taught me by their lives
the meaning of Christian discipleship.

Contents

Foreword

ON A VERY COLD DAY IN January 1993, I entered the warm bookstore on the campus of renowned Wheaton College near Chicago. We were there for a meeting of the Theological Commission of the World Evangelical Fellowship. I used a break between sessions to browse around and look at American literature. A book caught my attention. The author's name, with its Swabian suffix, sounded strangely familiar: Helmut Ziefle. As I skimmed through the book, I came across a very gripping biography. It talked about my hometown, Heilbronn. The author had attended the same high school (Gymnasium) that I did. The chapter about the destruction of the town by an Allied bombing attack on December 4, 1944, reminded me vividly of my grandparents' and my mother's descriptions of this phase of World War II.

Clearly, I had to get to know this man who was obviously a professor of German at Wheaton College. It was an interesting meeting on American soil. Also, the following summer, Helmut Ziefle, who directed the Wheaton College-sponsored academic summer program "Wheaton in Germany," was with a group of Wheaton College students at the Language Institute SIT in Tübingen. The Albrecht-Bengel-Haus was nearby, and the "Wheaton in Germany" students got a break from their German studies and met with students of theology at the Albrecht-Bengel-Haus. It was a new and open generation for whom this period of National Socialist crimes and the horrors of the war had long since been moved to the sidelines of world history. But they listened spellbound to the story of the German-American who had lived those years. The account of the terror of Hitler's regime left no one untouched. An intense discussion ensued. The gap between the generations had been bridged.

After his immigration to the United States in 1956, Helmut Ziefle assumed the task of a bridge builder for Christians in North America during the difficult phase of the postwar period. With his impressive family story, he could make clear for Americans how quickly people were taken in against their will by the pull of the terrifying events. When individuals got to know each other personally and felt how much each of them belonged together in a trustworthy imitation of Christ, confidence grew.

The author now makes available his moving story in a new, revised and expanded version. The generation of eyewitnesses from that time is vanishing quickly into the obscurity of the past. For this precise reason, this book is important for the coming generation. It is a document from the worst period of German history and is authenticated by both the realistic description of the persons involved and its straightforward truthfulness. While reading this account, one experiences a family whose members are convincing through their courage and assurance of faith. This book offers an impressive example of Christian existence in an extreme situation that can give the young generation confidence and perspective. Therefore, I wish this book many attentive readers.

—ROLF HILLE

Preface

MUCH HAS BEEN SAID AND written about Hitler and the Third Reich; the libraries can hardly hold the collected scholarship. "Why another such book?" the reader might ask. After all, we are informed, know the dates, and can recite the facts almost backward.

Yet, history does not happen outside of time and space. History is stories, individual stories of people, and the story of National Socialism includes the story of Christians who could not share that worldview. They were exposed to the persecution of party organs or even the Gestapo, and they had to experience—often daily—what it meant to be regarded as an "enemy of the people."

My parents, Georg and Maria Ziefle, belonged among those people. Their religious roots were in the Protestant church of the state of Württemberg, and there they were shaped, especially by the Evangelical Fellowship, which was founded and shaped by Johann Michael Hahn (1758–1819) *(Hahn'sche Gemeinschaft),* with its emphasis on edification and an uncompromising and living faith. Evangelical Fellowship supported the Protestant church but had its own fellowships and assembly halls in the states of Württemberg and Baden. Members worshiped in the Protestant church Sunday morning and in the Hahn'sche Fellowship in the afternoon. Hitler's attempt to gather believers in the national Christian movement, the German Christians, was not an option for them because Christ alone was their Lord and not the Führer.

Such a decision did not remain without visible consequences. It had an immediate effect on the upbringing of the children. My parents decided to oppose the Nazi slogans with a Christian way of life and to raise and instruct their four children in the faith as well as they could. They were not heroes, did not man the barricades, and were not taken to the concentration camp. Yet, they resisted passively and thus preserved for their children their exemplary model, guidance, and a home. Never did they join the Party in spite of the many advantages that membership would have brought them, and they never supported the Nazi Party in any way. This resistance caused them many a difficulty and led to many threats against them; yet, God gave them courage and firmness when other people showed them the cold shoulder.

Not until 1956, when I emigrated with my parents to the United States of America, did I really learn to understand and appreciate the extent and significance of their uncompromising daily decisions. The distance in time and space, and the viewpoint of a foreign culture that still looked upon Germany with considerable suspicion at that time, made me realize how thankful I had to be to my parents for their impartial lifestyle. Their testimony could thus make a small contribution to the much-implored international understanding.

Beyond that, I want to encourage readers in their faith through this book. Just as God has strengthened and protected my parents and their children during the Third Reich and the postwar years, He will also help His followers in other difficult situations.

"He who tries to cast off history will be killed by its ruins" (Klaus von Dohnanyi). Hitler's regime did not bring Germany the promised good fortune. Millions died as a result of the war, and shambles of broken dreams, betrayed illusions, and robbed youth remained. History must not be allowed to become mere facts of historiography; it must stay alive and have faces. Only then can we profit from the experiences of the old people. As a Chinese proverb says, "One must not study the past and the future in history, but the present."

With this hope, I remember my parents gratefully for their faithfulness and their example.

I am personally thankful that the Lord preserved my family and myself during these most difficult years of German history. After immigrating to the United States of America in 1956, I have come to appreciate more and more what it means to live in a free and open society. I am grateful to God and this great country for this unique opportunity.

Acknowledgments

THIS BOOK COULD NOT HAVE been written without invaluable help from two sources. First, I thank my siblings Reinhold and Ruth and especially my brother Kurt. Their memories of the events described in this book go back further, and I am very thankful for all additions and corrections. Special thanks also to Kurt for the photographs of Heilbronn after the bombing and many Ziefle family pictures. Kurt went on to become a professional photographer.

Furthermore, I rely on information from the book *Heilbronn—Die schwersten Stunden der Stadt* by Wilhelm Steinhilber.

I am indebted to these and other sources. The historical accuracy of this book has been verified.

In my Teutonic order, a youth will grow up which will frighten the world. I want a fierce, masterful, fearless and ferocious youth. It can't show any weakness or tenderness. The free and magnificent beast of prey must finally glow again from their eyes.

—Adolf Hitler

one

Autumn 1938

THE GOLD OF AUTUMN WAS magic to the German spirit. Gilded forests and mountains and the brisk air of southern Germany go out of their way to intoxicate its people with exuberance. But Maria Ziefle lay silent and tense in the darkened bedroom. She was staring with burning eyes at the ceiling, trying to find the sleep that evaded her.

Midnight. I lie in a warm bed next to my husband, and I shiver. Yet, it is not the cold of the night that creeps up in me—it's a death, a poison of which no one speaks, even if asked. Sounds are coming from the distance: the clapping of hands, male voices that sing to the stamping rhythm of the feet of Germany's pride and might, but worst, the steady beating of boots upon our cobblestone. I shiver.

The tentacles of the swastika are enclosing even little Sontheim. God, I am afraid—for my family and my country. My husband and I are helpless. And my three children, most of all, are helpless. God, give us grace and strength for whatever we must endure.

Shaking off her weariness from the sleepless night, Maria proceeded with her domestic routines—a morning trip to the butcher, the bakery, and finally the food market just around the corner. In the afternoon, she beat the living-room rug, washed bedding, and put a roast in the oven. In Heilbronn's gentle suburb of Sontheim, life still seemed ordinary.

Maria paused before the mirror in the upstairs corridor. Smoothing her brown hair back into the little bun at the nape of her neck, she stepped closer to check her work and hesitated. The blue eyes seemed faded. Her full cheeks had lost their lively ruddiness; her face was now drawn and lined. The gray dress only accentuated her aged appearance. This Nazi thing was wearing at her soul. She pulled herself together. She had to cook supper.

As she turned away with a sigh and began descending the stairs, the front door banged shut and footsteps clattered in the hall.

"Mama!" eleven-year-old Kurt exclaimed, breathless as he halted at the bottom of the steps. Maria couldn't help but smile at her second son's exuberance. Dark blond, athletic, and adventurous, wasn't he the near fulfillment of the Aryan dream?

"Mama, I joined the *Jungvolk* today! The meeting was great!" He paused expectantly, his bright face upturned toward his mother. He thought she would be pleased that he had joined the Young Folk, the junior division of the Hitler Youth, for youngsters ages ten to fourteen.

Halfway down the steps, she stared at her second child, and her smile faded. His dancing brown eyes and flushed innocence were untarnished, but the poison was now in her home.

"Aren't you happy I joined?" he asked finally.

Her throat tightened, but she pushed the words out stiffly. "Son, have you forgotten?"

"What do you mean, Mama?" He looked puzzled.

"No matter what you join"—her voice had regained its steady confidence—"remember that first you belong to Jesus."

Maria and Georg Ziefle had nurtured carefully their three children's sensitive spirits and had given them a solid foundation. Reinhold, the oldest and now thirteen; Kurt; and ten-year-old Ruth were the objects of their parents' frequent prayers and regular Bible teaching. The Creator and His written Word wielded unquestioned authority in the Ziefle household.

But the trusting minds of German children were now subject to strong, more adamant voices. One was extolling a new plan to restore the nation's shaken glory. For five years, the militarism of the "new liberation" movement had been propagated through radio, films, parades, and rallies. The voices spoke of a superior race, heroism for the Fatherland, and allegiance to the Führer. And they pushed God aside as a pathetic bystander or trimmed Him to fit the national desires.

Three years earlier, Julius Streicher, founder of *Der Stürmer* (*The Stormer*, a Nazi newspaper), told two hundred thousand youth at a festival on Hesselberg Mountain that Jesus Christ was "the greatest anti-Semite of all time." Urging them toward a united hatred of Jews, he warned, "Don't believe in priests as long as they defend people whom Christ called 'sons of the devil.'"

Such group pressure pulled a preadolescent such as Kurt in their grip. The disciplines, the parades, and the camaraderie appealed to him. And his life was not yet deeply rooted in God. When Hitler visited Heilbronn in 1935, Kurt had gone eagerly—against his parents' wishes—to watch the Führer's motorcade. Being a child, he was allowed to stand at the front of the crowd. The thrill of saluting the Aryan "messiah" with thousands of other bystanders left a strong impression on his mind. Innocently, he had embraced the hopes of Nazism.

Maria's supper preparations were more from habit than concentration that evening. The five Ziefles gathered eagerly for the meal as lukewarm rays of autumn sunset illuminated the dining room of their beige house. Kurt, pulling himself and his chair closer to the steaming roast beef, announced above the conversation, "From now on, we must all greet one another by saying, 'Heil Hitler!'"

Adolf Hitler travels through Sontheim on March 20, 1935.

The Ziefle family in 1938 (lower left to right; Maria, Ruth, Georg and upper left to right; Kurt and Reinhold).

The happy chatter ceased; silence gripped them as if it were a strangler. Four pairs of eyes turned toward Maria.

Her lips tightened as she glanced downward to avoid the pleading stares. "No, Kurt." Her voice was resolute. Maria lifted her eyes toward him and swallowed. "We do not salute a man in place of God. In this house we will continue to say, 'Grüss Gott,' 'May God greet you.' Is that understood?"

"Yes, Mama." He hung his head, trying to hide his embarrassment. Georg nodded his approval, and a smile of admiration reinforced his agreement. A man of modest physique, he was unmatched in his aggressive selling of sewing machines for the Singer Company of Heilbronn. Both friends and business colleagues respected his fine character, and his success had provided his family with a comfortable life. For spiritual wisdom, however, he often looked to his wife, who humbly received a flow of authoritative insight from the Lord whom they both followed.

Supper, though subdued, continued without further incident. Maria cleaned the kitchen, then finished the hem on a new skirt for Ruth. The children worked on school assignments, and Georg finished his newspaper. Bedtime was approaching, but first there must be *Dämmerstündle*.

The devotional time at dusk had been a ten-year tradition in this household. Centuries earlier, Martin Luther had stressed the importance of family togetherness and Christian education of children in the home; Georg and Maria regarded it as their divine commission.

Maria called the children to the second-floor living room, and the three crowded together onto the couch. Their parents each pulled up a chair facing them. Except for the dancing glow from the coal stove, the room was in darkness.

Maria began with a story from the Bible, told in her own inimitable way. The truths regarding the Almighty came easily to her, and no theologian could make men and women of Scripture seem more exciting and alive. The family joined in singing several hymns, Ruth accompanying them on the pump organ that stood in the corner of the room and Kurt playing his violin. Then, in their own darkened sanctuary, they knelt on the floor, and each of them prayed in turn.

As was her custom, Maria concluded with a German story of moral courage, of which she seemed to know dozens. This was her way of applying biblical truths to everyday life. The stories delighted the children, and they begged her to retell them again and again.

After Reinhold, Kurt, and Ruth proceeded to their beds, Maria and Georg also descended the stairway and entered their bedroom on the first floor. As her husband closed the door behind them, Maria slipped both arms around his waist and pulled him close to her. Alone with him in the darkness, her eyes glistened with moisture and her lips trembled.

"I'm afraid of the future," she began, her voice quivering. "I know that if we bring our problem to the Lord, He will work it out—but how? How can we save our children? Now Reinhold and Kurt are required to attend meetings where they are taught to hate God, the church—above all, Jews. And the Nazis make it so difficult for people who won't cooperate with them."

Georg stepped away for a moment to close the shutters. He shivered from the autumn coolness—or was it again from that strange chill that seemed to thrive in the darkness? He returned and kissed his wife. He spoke softly to avoid disturbing Ruth in the adjoining room.

"For thirteen years of marriage, I've devoted all my strength to providing for and protecting our family. I'm so proud of our sons and our daughter. I'll do anything to ensure that they follow our Savior."

As they prepared for bed he continued, "For now, we will have to let them attend the meetings. That is the law. But that is no problem for the Lord, is it? With His help, we will preserve them. I'm sure I pray many times a day, 'God, keep Reinhold, Kurt, and Ruth from being destroyed by the Nazi philosophies.'"

The couple climbed into bed and pulled the eiderdown comforter over them. Maria slid close and whispered, "If only more men in Germany prayed for their children as you do, this Nazi thing would never have begun."

"I don't think that I've done anything very great, but I know how important *your* influence is in our family. You are a good wife and mother, Maria, and your faith in the Lord has been rewarded with wonderful children who love you." Georg stopped for a moment. "I don't like to think negatively about my country; I love my homeland. But you and I both realize that bad things are going on. Yet, I think that whatever happens to the nation, God can keep our family. Don't you agree?"

Maria replied slowly, "I don't feel very confident about it, but I know you're right. God has never let us down."

"No use lying here worrying, then," Georg said with a comforting squeeze. "Let's get some rest." He kissed his wife heartily, then rolled over and fell asleep almost instantly.

Why can't I fall asleep so easily? God, I do trust that You will take good care of us. But the future is so uncertain. What will happen to us, to our children? I would not want them to face the hardships I faced as a child.

Thoughts of her early years raced through Maria's consciousness. Her mother had died when she was nine. A year later, her father remarried, but his new wife resented her stepchildren. Often, she sent them to school without breakfast, and during the winter they were not allowed to stay in the heated portion of the house.

At fifteen, Maria escaped from the oppressive home life and obtained work as a maid in Stuttgart. She thereby not only gained relief from her spiteful stepmother but also learned strict standards of housekeeping and became an accomplished seamstress. She would put these skills to good use in her own home. And she never forgot the misery of living in a home without love.

You've filled my heart with love for my children, heavenly Father. Don't let our family be torn apart by this Nazi regime. Keep our faith from wavering, whatever comes.

Home of Ziefle family on Ackermannstrasse 7/2, approximately 1937.

❧

Sewing machine sales had been very brisk that week, so Georg took Friday afternoon off to do some errands. "I'll be back in an hour, Mama," he called to his wife as he buttoned his jacket. Pulling the front door shut behind him and picking up the bike from the attached shed, he walked along the narrow path flanked on the left side by his house and Krauter's smaller attached house, and on the right side by farmer Bauer's fenced in backyard. He was heading for the Wohlwert (Woolworth) store in Heilbronn to purchase school supplies for the children.

Concern gripped Maria's heart as she ran from the kitchen and flung open the window on the second floor corridor. "Be careful! Too many strange things have been happening in the streets," she called.

He stopped immediately, looked up to her and assured her, "Don't worry, Mama, I'll watch out." Then he disappeared from her view as the path took a left turn toward Ackermannstrasse.

Jews in the Heilbronn area had been harassed increasingly by the Nazis during the previous months. Even the Ziefles' physician, Dr. Picard, had been receiving threatening phone calls. Now there was talk that Nazi "Brown Shirts" had been slashing tires of bicycles parked in front of Jewish-owned stores. Also, Woolworth's was said to be affected by it. Georg dismissed such talk as mere rumor.

As he pedaled down the street, Georg greeted neighbors and acquaintances. After fifteen minutes, he was parking his bicycle among a dozen others in front of Woolworth's.

❧

The door banged loudly behind him when Georg reentered the house after some time. Maria glanced up as he stamped into the kitchen. His face boiling with rage, he slammed his fist on the counter.

"I was in the Woolworth store only ten minutes—ten minutes! But when I came out, those nasty guys had slit both of my tires open!"

"Where is your bicycle now?" Maria's voice trembled slightly.

"I had to push it all the way home. Maria, this matter is going too far. If these scoundrels aren't stopped, they'll soon be doing even worse things to Jews in our town. God won't tolerate the persecution of innocent people!"

Nazis boycott Jewish businesses in Heilbronn, 1933.

"Papa, why don't we pray right now for our Jewish friends—and our children?" They knelt together by the couch.

As the couple rose from their knees several minutes later, their faith renewed, Reinhold and Kurt dashed into the house, their bags thumping against their legs.

"Well, boys, how was school today?" their father asked and greeted the two *Realschule* (junior high school) students with a smile. He hoped that they had not left their sister too far behind as they ran.

The boys looked at each other, hesitating. "We won't be having religious instruction any more. They've changed it to *Weltanschauungsunterricht*, instruction in the Nazi philosophy."

The parents gave each other a meaningful look. One of the teachers had urged them earlier, when their children were still attending grade school in Sontheim, to send their children to the new *Weltanschauungsunterricht,* but they had not given their permission. When they found out later that a major portion of the *Weltanschauungsunterricht* at the junior high school remained in the hands of principal Otterbacher, they could rest assured. Their children would get sound instruction from him.

Sunday was approaching, bringing with it another blow to the Ziefles. Until this time, school hours had been set aside each Wednesday for Nazi indoctri-

The Protestant church, Matthäuskirche, with view of choir, 1938.

nation and paramilitary drills. But beginning that month, attendance would also be required at Jungvolk rallies on the second Sunday of each month. On October 8, Reinhold and Kurt would be expected to miss church and attend the rally.

Conversation at the breakfast table that Sunday was subdued. Each person seemed to sense that conflict hovered over them. As she was clearing the table, Maria saw Kurt approach solemnly. Her heart sank as he said, "Mother, you know that I must go to the *Jungvolk* rally this morning. I'll be back in time for lunch." He turned and headed for the doorway.

Maria turned slowly toward Reinhold. "Are you going to go with him?"

"No, Mama. I'm a Christian, and I'm going to church."

Her erect German spirit barely restrained the tears and the embrace that she longed to give him. "That is good, son. That is good."

The four Ziefles walked quietly down Ackermannstrasse. Dwarfed by the huge red brick Ackermann yarn factories lining both sides of the street, Reinhold and Ruth strolled together wearing the new navy blue outfits that their mother had made. Maria was totally absorbed in thoughts about the missing member of their family.

In ten minutes, they had reached the only Protestant church in Sontheim. As they approached the steps of the Matthäuskirche on Lauffener Strasse 1, they noticed that Brown Shirts and Nazi sympathizers had gathered in front of their headquarters across the street to heckle the faithful. Loudly, some of them threatened to pelt the churchgoers with chunks of wood. The Ziefles mounted the steps silently, looking straight ahead.

Inside, the sanctuary seemed painfully barren. The Nazi regime discouraged church attendance. Of the congregation's two thousand members, only about twenty—mostly older women—were present on that particular morning. Even the beautiful ceiling fresco of Christ as the Lamb of God seemed stark and cold in the nearly empty building.

At 10:30, the church bells were rung and Pastor Brendle approached the lectern. He offered a short invocation and then announced the hymn, "Praise to the Lord, the Almighty, the King of Creation." The voices of the meager congregation, without organ accompaniment, echoed weakly from the walls of the edifice.

As she sang, Maria gazed with concern at the pastor. His muscular shoulders drooped as if he were much older than his forty years. His hair seemed

Pastor Theophil Brendle around 1942.

thinner, and sadness and frustrated concern had left their shadows around his eyes.

Three years earlier, when Theophil Brendle was still pastor in Vaihingen (Enz), he had criticized the Nazis in an article in his church bulletin for their sharp control of churches and betrayal of the nonintervention policy. He had quoted Paul in Galatians: ". . . false brethren unawares brought in, who came in privily to spy out our liberty which we have in Christ Jesus, that they might bring us into bondage." The Nazis retaliated by banning his bulletin for about six months.

Also unable to criticize the government from his pulpit in Sontheim lest he be arrested, Brendle nonetheless did all he could to ensure the spiritual welfare of his parishioners. He fought persistently to uphold the use of Scripture and religious instruction. The Gestapo kept him under close scrutiny, and school officials criticized him continually. Kurt once saw two policemen grab Pastor Brendle by his arms and drag him from the schoolyard when he wanted to continue to give religious instruction.

As the hymn drew to a close, the blare of trumpets and raucous voices singing Hitler's songs savagely invaded the quiet sanctuary. Nevertheless, Pastor Brendle climbed self-consciously to the pulpit to deliver the sermon. After an uncertain moment, he began to preach, but the parishioners could hardly hear him.

Georg leaped from the pew, his face red with anger. Maria desperately grasped the tail of his coat and pulled him down to his seat.

"Don't do anything now," she whispered urgently, "for our family's sake— and the church's." Her fingers still clutched his woolen jacket. Georg remained in the seat, his hands trembling and his lips pressed together.

The pastor dutifully continued his sermon, although he could barely hear himself above the loud songs and shouts outside the windows. His unflinching self-control was the greatest sermon he had delivered in months. Frequent oral treatises on complex orthodoxies only bewildered his flock. Today, their shepherd's message reached their hearts, although hardly a word of it was audible.

Ruth's merrily swinging braids did little to lighten the Ziefles' solemnity as they walked home. Their feelings needed little discussion. Even Maria's usual emotional control was visibly shaken.

As their children walked on ahead, Georg growled in a low voice, "When will it end, Mama? My patience is nearly gone. There's been so much tension at work, in our home, and now—in church!"

"I wish I had an answer." Maria's eyes gazed far ahead. "God knows. But somehow that really doesn't seem enough, does it?"

Kurt was waiting for the family near the entrance when they arrived home. Beaming, he exclaimed, "Let me tell you what we did at *Jungvolk* this morning!" The family walked silently toward the door.

Aerial view of Sontheim from the South, taken August 13, 1933. Protestant Matthäuskirche in foreground to the right, Catholic St. Martinuskirche in center, and buildings of Ackermann Yarn Factory with smokestacks in background.

Main Street with view of Matthäuskirche in 1934.

Adolf Hitler! We are united with you alone! On this earth we believe in Adolf Hitler alone. We believe that National Socialism is the sole redeeming faith for our nation.

—Dr. Robert Ley,
head of the National Socialist Labor Front

two

October 1938

MARIA RESTRAINED HER determined stride as she approached the Neckar River, which angled across the northern edge of Sontheim. Here she wanted to slow her pace after a busy morning of errands and housework. The ground was mottled with fallen leaves, and early afternoon sunlight danced warmly through the half-barren tree branches. She inhaled deeply in the crisp breeze that blew over the river. This was a welcome respite from the daily routine with its busy neighborhood and necessary therapy for her phlebitis.

But these regular walks were, more importantly, a time for communion with her Lord, a sacred hour to muse upon the Scripture that she had read carefully as she ate her lunch of soup and bread. And now she had so much to consider and to tell her Master.

Earlier in the year, during the summer when it was very hot, Maria's children had asked her to go swimming with them. When she went into the water, her feet seemed to become heavier and heavier, and she had such cramps in her legs, along with severe hemorrhaging, that she went to see a woman doctor in Heilbronn. The doctor examined her and announced, "Frau Ziefle, you are expecting."

Upon hearing this news Maria had been frightened, because she had given birth to her youngest child eleven years earlier and had not expected another one. But now, at forty years of age, Maria was once again pregnant. Also, everyone talked about Hitler and the possibility of war. Concerned about all of this now, she asked the Lord that the child would not be born during the war, because the thought that this might happen terrified her. And, indeed, the child could still enter this world in peacetime.

Soon after learning she was pregnant, Maria had made an appointment with her family physician. "Well, Frau Ziefle, you are right," Dr. Picard had announced with a grin across his usually serious face. "You are going to have a baby—probably in early April, just before Easter."

"I don't know how Georg is going to take this," Maria had replied slowly as she stared out the window of the office. "In fact, I almost wish for the child's sake that this baby wouldn't have to be born. These are not pleasant times for a little one to enter the world."

"But life is never easy, is it?"

"Do you know, Doctor, that I have dreamed three times in the last month that I was giving birth to a child? Each time, I seemed to hear the voice of God assuring me that all would be well, and the child would be protected. And I'm sure it was God speaking to me."

"Your faith amazes me, Frau Ziefle. You realize there can be complications for a pregnant woman of your age? But you are strong and healthy—aside from your phlebitis—and with such faith, who knows, maybe you will give birth to an Isaac! His mother was ninety, you know."

"I know, Doctor."

In spite of Maria's misgivings, Georg had shown almost boyish delight at the prospect of another child. For him, it was a happy diversion from the mounting pressures that seemed to touch every aspect of their lives. Georg's excitement had greatly eased the burden on Maria's mind.

Also prominent in her thoughts this afternoon was the coming weekend. Maria had recently written a letter to her sister and brother-in-law, Berta and Christian Hayer of Maubach, asking if the Ziefles could spend the weekend at their home. The reply had not yet come. The family needed to get away. The pressure of the threats and angry looks of the Nazis was mounting slowly, and a weekend retreat from their surroundings would give Georg and Maria a chance to untangle their thoughts.

Lord, we need that reply from Berta. It's such a small thing for You to hurry a letter through the mail. We need to breathe the peaceful air of Maubach, to be assured that You are the God who gives peace. You have promised so clearly that

View of Sontheim with *"der Steg,"* a footbridge in foreground, as seen from walking path across Neckar River. It connects the small towns of Sontheim and Böckingen, both of which were incorporated with Heilbronn.

View of Sontheim from across Neckar River.

You will take care of this baby inside me. Please, give me the same hope for the rest of my family.

What Maria couldn't know at this time was that the pregnancy, with all of its complications, would almost cost her life.

Maria's concentration turned to the traffic on Heilbronner Strasse (now named Kolpingstrasse) while she attempted to cross the busy thoroughfare. As she reached the other side and entered Ackermannstrasse, a sense of something strong and bright surged within her. Her spirit responded to the Presence, and for a moment her steps seemed lighter, and her shoulders straightened with youthful vigor.

"Heil Hitler!"

Maria turned her head to see Herr Z___, her neighbor, approaching on his bicycle. She nodded and smiled. The man dropped his salute slowly and wagged his head disapprovingly. The neighbors had been increasingly insistent that the Ziefles salute in the Führer's name. Z___ might report the incident to Herr W___, the highest-ranking Nazi in the neighborhood. Maria resolutely put the incident out of her mind.

As she turned toward her house, Maria ran optimistically toward the brown steel mailbox by the door. She flipped the top open and slipped her fingers in. There was an envelope. Her heart pounding, she jerked it out and gave the handwriting a quick glance. It was Berta's irregular script!

She hurried through the doorway and up the stairs, tearing open the envelope as she went. Maria settled herself eagerly on the couch in the living room to read:

Dear Maria,

I was so happy to hear from you again! I agree that these are troublesome times, but things are much quieter in Maubach, I'm sure. Christian was wondering yesterday when we would be able to visit with you and Georg again. We will look forward to seeing you Friday night when. . . .

Maria stopped with tears in her eyes. Words were not necessary. Her heart expressed to the heavens all of the appreciation she felt. That brightness surged afresh in her.

On Friday, Maria hurried through her housekeeping duties to prepare for the weekend trip. She wanted to bake a cake after lunch and pack the suitcase so that the family would not be delayed in leaving. By foregoing her afternoon stroll, she finished the baking and had time for a short nap before the children arrived. And that was good because carrying a child at her age taxed her energy.

As the three young Ziefles returned, Maria laid a large brown suitcase on her bed and called to them, "Children, change out of your school clothes. As soon as you're finished, bring the outfits you will wear to church on Sunday so I can pack them."

One by one, they delivered their clothes to her bedroom. As they arrived, Maria assigned each child a job: "Ruth, peel the potatoes for supper. Reinhold, run to the fabric shop to purchase the sewing notions that Berta requested. And Kurt, clean the ashes from the heating stove, the oven in the kitchen, and the water boiler in the laundry."

When Georg arrived from work, the potatoes and sausage were boiling and the suitcase was ready. The five Ziefles ate more quickly than usual; they all wanted to leave for Maubach as early as possible. As soon as they finished eating, each of them carried the dishes into the kitchen. Maria and Ruth washed them while Georg prepared the car and Reinhold and Kurt ran to the home of the Krauters, who shared the Ziefles' cellar, and asked them to watch the house in their absence. The three children clambered eagerly into the back seat of their green BMW automobile, a two seater with a luggage compartment in the back with enough room for not only the luggage but also the children. Because the train service to Maubach was poor, the family always traveled there by car. They had not seen their aunt and uncle since March, when they had left Sontheim to avoid the Austria annexation referendum. Maubach was always one of their favorite places to visit. The sun was a bright ball, low in the west, as their vehicle droned past the last scattered houses of Sontheim. Only thirty miles separated Sontheim and Maubach, so no one settled down very much.

"I'm going to help Uncle Christian in his blacksmith shop tomorrow," Reinhold declared.

"You can work in that smelly old place if you want to," Kurt retorted, "but

I'm going to play with Waldi." Waldi was a bushy, black-haired mongrel that the children adored.

"Mama, why can't we have a dog too?" Ruth asked as usual when the subject of Waldi arose.

Maria smiled and shook her head. "Where would we keep one? Our yard is so small; we hardly have space for our little garden."

"But we could get a little Dachshund and keep him in the house," suggested Kurt.

"Oh, no. No puppies in the house! But do you know what? I think we may be able to have a little surprise in the spring!" Maria and Georg glanced at each other, trying to contain their amusement.

"Do you mean a pet, Mama?" Ruth almost jumped over the front seat in her excitement.

"Well, you *might* call it that," Maria answered thoughtfully.

"A cat!" exclaimed Kurt. "But if it's as lazy as the Krauters' old Erhardt, I don't want it."

"Oh, it's much nicer than a cat—and more useful too." Maria was enjoying the guessing game, and Georg chuckled quietly as he drove.

"Is it a rabbit?" Reinhold joined in the game, also puzzled. "Or maybe a chicken?"

"A chicken?" Ruth looked at him with her nose wrinkled up. "What kind of pet is that?"

"I know," Georg interrupted. He patted his wife's knee to assure her that he wasn't about to spill her secret. "I bet it's a piggy! What could be more useful than that? And your mother said it would be a surprise."

The children glanced at each other and shrugged their shoulders in bewilderment. Reinhold quipped, "I'll bet we'll be the only family in Sontheim with a piggy for a pet!"

They all laughed and began to discuss names for their future "piggy."

The Ziefles arrived at Maubach in less than an hour. Eager to start their activities early—their cousins, Gerhard and Hans, would have a full day planned—the children went to bed quickly. The adults were then free to discuss their concerns over the troubles rising around them. It was best not to bring up such subjects in front of the young ones because one of them might innocently quote a parent's opinions to a schoolteacher or neighbor—a dangerous mistake.

The midnight tramping of boots and the harassment of good people by Brown Shirts had not yet infected Maubach. Although Georg and Maria were not about to ignore their troubles, the two days away from Sontheim were a happy retreat from their daily anxieties. The warm greetings between neighbors and the tranquil orderliness of well-kept farmland invigorated their fatigued souls. As the Ziefles awakened Saturday morning, they savored the gentle sounds of this rural village. Sontheim's early-morning rumbling from the Ackermann mill and the bustling traffic on Heilbronner Strasse were out of sight and sound. Rather, one's ears were soothed by the pastoral chorus of feasting pigs, egotistical roosters, and restless milk cows awaiting the farmer and his pail. This was music in their ears.

The Ziefle children worked and played with their cousins, relishing the simple delights of searching for the hens' eggs and kicking a soccer ball down the little-used streets. Georg enjoyed the release of physical work as he assisted Christian in the blacksmith shop. Maria basked in the warm gentleness of caring for the livestock with Berta. The contented grunting of the pigs and the gentle clucking of the hens helped to soothe Maria's tense mind. She mused over her predicament. She enjoyed life in the country to the fullest.

Lord, how much I wished that we could live in such a peaceful and happy place. Here people love and trust each other. We have a nice house and a car, but the people of Maubach are rich in kindness. Whatever happens around us in Sontheim, please keep love in our family.

A highlight of the weekend for Georg and Maria was the time of concerned prayer with Berta and Christian on Saturday night. It helped to dissipate Georg and Maria's sense of aloneness, which had almost overwhelmed them in the preceding weeks.

As the Hayers and the Ziefles walked to the church on Sunday morning, they were joined on the street by many other families. Suddenly, not to be alone had seemed strange to the Ziefles, who had already become used to the fact that worship and all other spiritual fellowship was now the target of persecution. As they neared the building, Maria tensed, then forced herself to relax. She smiled at herself—there were no Brown Shirts here.

The assembly room in the school where the worship service was held was simple. So were the people and their pastor. Their singing was unrefined but vigorous. The sermon was easily understandable. Georg and Maria were heartened by the assurance that love and faith still existed in Germany.

The rest of the day progressed all too quickly. Not wanting to return home late, Georg, Maria, and the children ate an early supper with their relatives and headed for Sontheim before six o'clock. They reached their home as the sun was setting but with their optimism rekindled. No insurmountable problems seemed to be on the horizon.

༄

As if the weekend had been some kind of magical potion, the next few days were unusually placid. Kurt talked little of the *Jungvolk* meeting, the neighbors seemed more cordial, and Georg's sales were exceptional. Even Maria began to think that maybe life was on the swing back toward normal.

But the pendulum swung back viciously on the following Friday afternoon. Maria was in the kitchen, cheerfully ironing Georg's pants, when she heard the clatter of shoes on the tile of the foyer below. She stepped through the living room toward the stairway and caught a glimpse of the clock on the china closet—2:30. *Much too early for the children,* she thought.

"Maria!" A woman's frenzied scream rang up the steps. "Maria, they've taken Wilhelm!"

Maria rushed into the corridor just as her sister-in-law, Paula Glaser, came stumbling to the top of the stairs, shrieking hysterically. Maria ran toward Paula, her arms outstretched. The woman collapsed against her, sobbing fitfully.

Holding her firmly, Maria led her into the living room and sat her gently in a chair at the large wooden table. She pulled the adjoining chair closer and held the woman's head on her shoulder, stroking her dark brown hair. Paula's entire body convulsed with each violent sob. After a few minutes, Paula began to quiet down.

"Who has taken Wilhelm—and where?" Maria questioned between Paula's sobs.

"The Gestapo"—her speech was broken by rhythmic, jerky whimpers— "committed him to Weissenhof, the mental hospital."

"Weissenhof? Wilhelm is not insane! There must be some mistake."

"A Nazi official came to my door just before noon, Maria, and told me. He claimed Wilhelm had suddenly gone mad. I told him that was impossible."

Paula continued, but her sobbing increased again. "He looked at me as if I were some child and said, 'Frau, you are wrong. While talking to his foreman,

Wilhelm and Paula Glaser in Heilbronn after World War II.

your husband called Hitler a scoundrel. The foreman informed the Kupfer-Asbest (copper-asbestos factory) management of this, and they called the Gestapo. We had no choice but to consider him insane.'" She laid her face on the table and wept helplessly. Maria waited quietly; instinctively, her thoughts turned to the Almighty.

Why do You allow the good men to suffer? Why do the godless rule our land? Am I supposed to walk into Hitler's office and slap his hands? God, You must stop this horror—only You can. If You do not stop this, we may all die.

Her lips pressed together rigidly, and her own eyes filled with tears. Inwardly, Maria screamed, *I'm helpless, Lord! I'm just one woman against this colossal power! She calmed herself. I should have known that this week was too good to be true. But how was I to expect something like this? My own brother behind bars!*

Paula began to regain control. Maria cradled the quivering hands in her own, blinked away her own tears, and looked directly into the tear-stained face. "Did you go to the Kupfer-Asbest factory to find out what really happened?" she asked curiously.

"I went right away. I found Wilhelm's foreman, but he seemed hardly bothered by the matter. He confirmed that Wilhelm had called Hitler a scoundrel. Shortly after Wilhelm said it, the management called the Gestapo; they came and wrestled him to the floor and took him away to the hospital.

"Then—and I've never heard anyone speak so coldly—he sneered, 'Everyone must be sacrificed for the Party. You should be glad you're rid of that traitor. He's lucky he's still alive.' Right after that, I came straight here."

Maria thought of her childhood when she and her brothers and sisters had lived under the oppression of their stepmother. She remembered the cold winter nights in their home in the Baar (a rough, elevated plain located between the Southern Black Forest and the Swabian Alb) and how she had piled blankets on Wilhelm and the others to keep them warm. He was now thirty-six, but she knew that he needed her just as much now as he had when he was only five.

"We have to see him; that's the first thing we must do," Maria began matter-of-factly, trying to contrive a plan as she spoke. Her face brightened. "That's it! We'll go through Doctor Wagner. He's a high official in the Nazi Party; Georg knows him very well. I'm sure he will help us."

"Maria, I'm so glad I have you to help me." Paula's reddened eyes glimmered with fresh hope.

"Don't lean on me, Paula. Lean on God. He is the only One who will never fail—even if our circumstances seem hopeless. And right now, I don't know how even He can get us out of this mess. But He will."

Paula nodded meekly.

When Georg arrived home and received the news, he sat in stunned silence. The mounting inhumanities of the local Nazis continually angered him, but suddenly it had all become very personal. He and Wilhelm were good friends. He paced about the living room, shaking his fists and muttering, "Animals! Germany is being governed by animals!" Paula gladly accepted the Ziefles' invitation to spend the night. *Dämmerstündle,* especially, would be a great encouragement to her. There was also another guest for the devotional time that evening—Fritz R___, who was a master baker and confectioner at the local bakery. Of late, he had become a frequent visitor at the late evening event, always giving a jaunty knock at the door and entering without waiting for an answer.

Fritz was Catholic; through his contacts with Maria at the bakery and his eventual visits to the home, he had embraced Christ as his own Lord. Now he enjoyed the opportunity to fellowship with the Ziefles; he would pray with them and take his turn reading aloud from the Bible that Georg had given him. He seemed to view Maria as a second mother, and she enjoyed the opportunity to give him advice and pray for him. As they prayed for Wilhelm that night, they also voiced their concerns for their nation. None of them wanted to see Germany fall into moral decay.

The next day, Georg visited Dr. Wagner at his office and asked him to secure permission for them to visit Wilhelm. Wagner, a longtime business acquaintance of Georg's, was happy to oblige. By the next Friday, Georg, Maria, and Paula received clearance to go to Weissenhof.

The scene at the hospital was beyond their imaginations. Wilhelm had become a slobbering, grunting, writhing madman. He did not even recognize his wife. The three stared in horror through the bars of the cell. Finally, Paula broke the silence, no longer able to stifle her wails. The woman's knees began to falter, so Maria and Georg grabbed her arms and led her to a nearby chair.

"Take me home," she whispered through white lips. Her eyes stared blankly. "It's hopeless; there's nothing I can do for him now." She held her head, a long wail again escaping her.

Georg and Maria stared at each other in bewilderment. Maria motioned for him to join her a few feet down the corridor from Paula. "Papa, something tells me that things are not as they seem," Maria whispered. "I think they have done something to Wilhelm to make him seem crazy. He has been too stable a man to suddenly act like this."

"I felt the same way as soon as I saw him. If Wilhelm were insane now, we'd have noticed some warning signs before this. I'll see if Wagner can get me some answers perhaps."

Georg made several telephone calls to Dr. Wagner, attempting to find out the truth. Unaccompanied by Paula, Georg and Maria visited Wilhelm five times. They became increasingly concerned as they saw his physical condition deteriorating. Wilhelm's life seemed to be in jeopardy.

The doctor finally surrendered to Georg's relentless calling and pressured the physicians at Weissenhof for an answer. The Ziefles' suspicions proved correct. Before each visit from his relatives, Wilhelm was forced to swallow pills, which induced his irrational behavior. Nothing was wrong with him—except that he had told the truth about the Führer. But the Nazis had no intentions of releasing Wilhelm. Maria would pray and weep much for her brother in the ensuing months.

☙

As the days of autumn grew steadily colder, so did the attitudes of some of the pro-Nazi neighbors. Each afternoon as Maria took her stroll, she encountered one or more acquaintances who saluted zealously and snapped, "Heil Hitler." She always smiled and nodded in return, but each time, their critical stares were more incisive. Herr Z___, who was also block warden and collected donations for the Nazi Party, was the worst. His salutes were drenched with mockery. And, of course, Herr W___, the highest-ranking Nazi, always eyed her with suspicion.

Such encounters were proving to be too much for Maria, so she resorted to the cover of darkness for her regular stroll. With Georg at her side, she walked up and down the upper Ackermannstrasse for fifteen or twenty minutes, getting as much exercise and fresh air as possible. These were good times for the couple to discuss things privately. But even in the dark, deserted street, they spoke only in whispers; they were now aliens, even in their own neighborhood.

As the weeks passed, the swelling of life inside Maria began to make itself plain. Thus far, the camouflage of her bulky coat had kept the matter secret from people, but she wondered how soon they would begin to notice.

The three children, still anticipating their "piggy," were also unaware until one afternoon late in November. They were outside in the backyard, busying

Fritz R___ in 1973.

themselves with building a little barn for the future pet. Kurt came into the kitchen to get a drink. As he gulped the water, he observed his mother as she arched backward, trying to stretch after stooping over her baking. Eyeing her expanding abdomen, he suddenly brightened up and blurted, "Mama, are you going to have a baby? Is that what you meant by a 'surprise'?"

She grinned sheepishly and nodded.

Kurt whirled and ran downstairs and out the door. "Reinhold! Ruth! We'd better get rid of this piggy barn. We're getting something much better—Mama's going to have a baby!"

The other two children dropped their work and ran behind Kurt into the house and upstairs to the kitchen. They crowded around their mother, cheering and asking questions. Reinhold appeared slightly embarrassed that his younger brother had discovered the secret before he did. Kurt always seemed to be the bold one.

At the age of thirteen, Kurt was enrolled in confirmation class at the Matthäuskirche. Many of the teenagers in the class were there against their will; deep-rooted religious traditions still influenced parents in the early Hitler years, although most of the men no longer attended church. The children respected their parents' wishes and attended the classes, but, for most of them, their hearts were far from the catechism.

Pastor Brendle attempted desperately to teach his beliefs to the children, although most of them were not even faintly interested. They reacted with scorn and violence. The boys, especially, jeered him and encouraged the girls to join them in their misbehavior. Eventually, they were throwing student Bibles and catechisms around in the classroom and overturning tables and chairs. Brendle tolerated them as best he could; complaints to their parents or the authorities would be useless.

In spite of Kurt's shallow regard for God's truth, he remained firm in his respect for authority. Concerned by the taunts of his classmates, he attempted to set a good example by helping the pastor pick up the books and set the furniture back in its place. Instead, this action only antagonized his peers.

"Don't you dare go home today!" one of the ringleaders growled to Kurt as the class was being dismissed. "We're going to beat you up."

Unperturbed, Kurt eyed him coolly and replied, "I'm not afraid of you. When are you going to start acting civilized?"

"You just wait!" the bully snapped as he whirled around and stepped to-

Matthäuskirche (the Protestant church, left) with Ackermannstift (educational center for church functions such as confirmation classes, kindergarten, etc., right) where Kurt encountered the boys who wanted to beat him up. (Photo from approximately 1912.)

ward the door. Outside, he gathered five of his cronies and waited at the gate in front of the church.

Also helping Pastor Brendle was a girl named Hilde. Kurt worked, somewhat bashfully, with her to finish cleaning the classroom. They bade their pastor goodbye and strolled out the door together. In front of them stood six of their classmates with their jaws and fists clenched. Undaunted, Kurt marched straight toward the group with Hilde close behind. He stiff-armed the first boy's chest and grunted, "Get out of my way!" The two walked past the rest of the bullies without another word. Kurt told his parents nothing of the incident.

Embarrassed by the episode, the six Lutheran boys gathered a group of their Catholic friends to help teach Kurt a lesson. The next week, after he and Hilde had cleaned up the room and walked outside, they found themselves facing ten boys, all of them trying to look as fierce as possible. Without hesitating, Kurt and Hilde quickened their pace and stared straight ahead. The silent gang members raised their fists. The two passed through the pack, but the boys stood as if they were frozen.

This time Kurt couldn't restrain himself when he arrived home. "Mama, when Hilde and I left confirmation class, ten bullies were waiting to beat me up. We just walked right through them, and it was as—as if someone cast a spell on them. They didn't even move!"

Maria was glad for the chance to show that God was working in the life of the son for whom she was most concerned. "Don't you think that maybe God protected you? Maybe He sent angels to hold those boys so that they couldn't harm you."

Embarrassed at the thought, Kurt turned and moved away. "Maybe, Mama. Maybe." Maria smiled. The Spirit was using even miracles to keep her son's weak faith from evaporating.

Her thoughts jumped quickly back to her encounter with Fritz R___ just that morning in the bakery. For two weeks, he had not stopped in for *Dämmerstündle*, so today she had made a point of asking him about it. He mysteriously changed the subject and never answered her question. She was concerned about the troubled expression on his face.

Lord, maybe Your angels need to give Fritz a miracle too.

Soon after supper, a loud knock sounded at the door. Reinhold ran to answer. A few seconds later, his voice rang up the stairs, "Papa, it's Fritz! He wants to talk to you!" Georg disappeared down the steps.

Fritz kept his eyes toward the floor as Georg approached him. "Herr Ziefle, I've come to return your Bible—I won't be needing it anymore. I've been considering my future, and the only way that I can see opportunity for success is with the Nazis. They would not want me to have this." He thrust the Bible into Georg's hands, whirled, and bolted out the door. Georg did not even get his mouth open to answer.

"Maria!" Georg called as he trudged up the stairs. His voice heavy with disappointment, he held up the Bible as evidence. "We've lost Fritz, Maria." Maria hung her head and stood wringing her hands.

God be merciful to Fritz. If it weren't for God's promise of protection, I would almost wish that the baby would not live through delivery. I don't want him to have to face the Nazis and lose his faith like Fritz.

❧

All of these worries that surrounded the family only aggravated Maria's physical problems. As her delivery date drew closer, she became increasingly weak. Housework was an exhausting trial, and the rounds to the stores for groceries became nearly impossible.

It was now early March, and she had only a month to go. With Georg's coaxing and assistance, Maria painfully continued her nightly walks. Supporting her valiantly with his arms, Georg helped Maria as she dragged her feet toward Staufenbergstrasse then back to the house.

One evening after they had hardly returned home and entered the living room to call the children for *Dämmerstündle,* they heard frantic knocking at the door. Georg quickly descended the stairs to answer. "Paula! What is the matter?" he exclaimed as he opened the door to his sister-in-law.

"Wilhelm can come home! He's being released!" she exclaimed as she stepped into the hallway, shivering with excitement. She paused for a moment then rushed up the stairs.

"Maria! Did you hear?" she said breathlessly. "Wilhelm can come home tomorrow!"

Maria was silent. Seated on the couch, she held her hands close to her face; her eyes were already glistening with tears. She motioned for Paula to sit beside her. Paula quickly came to her side, and they wept in each other's arms.

The next morning, Georg, Maria, and Paula stepped nervously out of their car and approached the main entrance of the mental hospital. As they stepped through the doorway and entered the lobby, a bent, emaciated figure approached them. The tall, once-strong Wilhelm whom they remembered was almost unrecognizable. Paula ran toward him and embraced and kissed him; they had not touched for six months.

Wilhelm finally stepped away from his wife and approached his sister and brother-in-law. Weakly, he placed his arms around them. "Thank you." His voice was thin and raspy. "Thank you for helping us, for getting my release."

Maria sniffed quietly and squeezed him harder. "We worked, but God made the way. It's a miracle you are even alive."

"You're right, sister. You're so right."

Slowly, the four made their way back to the car. Hardly able to comprehend his new freedom, Wilhelm sat and stared at the countryside as they drove toward Sontheim. The others were too happy to speak. In a short while, the four had gathered around the dining-room table at the Ziefles' house.

Wilhelm, unsteady from his long ordeal, held his coffee cup with both hands. "When the Gestapo arrested me at the factory," he began, "the officers grabbed me and threw me down on the floor. They held me down while one of them kicked me several times. I screamed in pain, and one of them shouted to the workers who watched, 'See, he is insane!'

"As soon as I was brought to Weissenhof, they tied me in a straitjacket and pushed me into the cell. I was already in great pain and could hardly move. One of the officers began describing what a terrible crime I had committed against the Fatherland and promised that I would be severely punished. I told him, 'You can't make me feel guilty for telling the truth. I demand that you let me go.'

"The men became furious. One of them shouted, 'You *Schweinehund!* We'll teach you who is in authority!' The officers pulled me to my feet and began to beat me with their fists until I was bruised all over. They threw me against the wall and I collapsed. Then they just walked out and locked the cell door.

"I hardly slept that night because of the pain. The next morning two aides came in and dragged me to a surgical room. They strapped me onto a table and, without giving me any anesthesia, they—" Wilhelm stared into his coffee. His voice barely audible, he murmured, "They sterilized me." (Dr. Joos, the chief medical officer at the Weissenhof who did this brutal operation, committed suicide before the American military government could remove him from his office.) "They didn't want my 'bad genes' to be passed on." He sat silent for a few moments as the horror dawned on his three listeners.

"It was several days before the pain was gone. When I finally felt strong again, I told some aides, 'Someday, you will pay for what you have done to me.' They became very angry and beat me. I still don't remember many details after that. I finally became so sick and weak that I was sure I would die. I had not been a very good Christian before, but I cried out to God as never before and asked Him to help me and to free me from the torture. I spent much time talking to God after that. It was the only way I kept my sanity."

Georg interrupted. "Do you have any idea why they finally released you?"

"I'm not sure what prompted them to do it, but two days ago a pair of aides came to my cell and escorted me to the director's office. The director ordered me to sit down. Then for a long time he sat writing at his desk, totally ignoring me.

"Finally, he glared at me and shouted, 'Glaser, insulting our beloved Führer is a detestable crime! You deserve to be exterminated.' I was certain that my life was over then. I just stared at the floor.

"The director became even angrier and screamed, 'Are you sorry for what you did?'

"I was speechless. I didn't understand why he would ask me that. Suddenly, I sensed a voice telling me not to offend this man. So I told him that I was sorry.

"He said, 'If you promise not to criticize the great Führer anymore, you will be a free man in two days.' I gladly promised him that—at least I won't criticize him publicly!"

"I believe it was a miracle," declared Maria. "Let's thank God for it right now."

All four of them were overflowing with praise as they voiced their gratitude to the Deliverer. Maria listened with deep joy to Wilhelm and Paula. The ordeal had brought them both closer to God.

Maria's spirit was strengthened through her brother's homecoming, but her body continued to weaken. Later that week, she had so little stamina that the doctor admitted her to the hospital for rest and intravenous feeding. Dr. Picard, who stood by his Jewish wife, had been barred from his practice, so Maria was under the care of Dr. Schramm, who lived near the Ziefle home. The baby was not due for three weeks.

Maria had lost much weight, and her family and friends became alarmed at her condition. But despite the strain on her body, her spirit was resolute. Ernst Veigel, a Christian friend, noted, "Frau Ziefle, there is no question in my mind you will survive. Through your eyes I see much faith and fight in you. You are a strong woman."

The wait was painful for both mind and body. Maria felt helpless as she had to lie in bed, unable to be home guiding her children and aiding her husband. Even Georg began to look a bit tired. *He needs some of my gruel that he likes so well,* she told herself.

But God stood by her. She regained enough strength so that she was allowed to return home to await her child's birth. On April 2, 1939, Palm Sunday, Maria felt the first contractions beginning. Georg soon called for the midwife. Five minutes before midnight, the Ziefle children had a new, somewhat skinny but healthy brother. They all agreed on the name Helmut and shared great ambitions to spoil him in every way possible. Maria's time and thoughts were now concentrated on caring for her new child. And Georg proudly told everyone of his little Helmut.

Life and innocence were cause for celebration in the Ziefle house. The hatred and suspicion that surrounded them were forgotten temporarily.

Maria holding up her youngest son Helmut on Ackermannstrasse.

The Jews are a parasitic race that lives in the culture of healthy nations like mold. There is only one remedy for that: Make a cut and get rid of them, ruthless and cold.

—Joseph Goebbels
Minister of Propaganda of the Reich

three

Reichskristallnacht (Crystal Night) 1938

"THIS IS A BLACK DAY FOR HEILBRONN!" Principal Otterbacher sighed when he watched with his class from the schoolyard of the Junior High School the synagogue that was burning in the distance. In the early morning hours of November 1938, the huge dome had collapsed into the interior of the desecrated Jewish House of God.

And yet this was not the only terror attack that the Nazis had carried out against Jewish citizens and establishments in and around Heilbronn during the so-called *Kristallnacht.*

The anger of the agitated mob was also directed against Dr. Picard, the Ziefles' family doctor, who lived in Sontheim, Lauffener Strasse 12, with his wife Gertrude, whose maiden name was Grünfelder. Dr. Picard himself was not Jewish, but he had always participated faithfully in the congregational life of his wife.

When he was ordered to leave his wife if he didn't want to be treated as a Jew, he stood by her side. For quite some time already, he had had to pay the consequences for this decision. He could practice medicine only on a limited basis. His two sons, Gustav and Helmut, who were born in Sontheim and were medical doctors just like their father, had emigrated to the United States in 1936 and 1937, respectively. The situation became more and more critical. Therefore, Dr. Picard tried to sell some of his household goods privately. This was not easy because under penalty of heavy sentences it was forbidden for

Burning synagogue of Heilbronn, November 10, 1938.

Dr. Julius Picard with his wife Gertrude after 1918.

Germans to buy anything from Jews. Yet, the medical doctor of many years knew his patients and was sure whom he could trust.

"Dr. Picard asked me today," Georg whispered to Maria, "if I would buy a closet from him so that he will get some money for his passage to America." Maria approved, of course, although the thought that she would lose her old doctor in this way broke her heart. The piece of furniture had to be brought into the house in secret under the cover of darkness because during the day the Nazis patrolled frequently in front of Dr. Picard's entrance.

And now *Kristallnacht!* An angry mob positioned itself in front of the Picards' house, threw stones at it, and forced their way into the house. The couple had no means of defending themselves against the brutal men. Gertrude was in bed with the flu and was manhandled so badly with staghorns taken from the wall that she sustained very serious injuries and could not move any more for twenty-four hours. Also, her husband suffered severe wounds in the face and on the eye and collapsed, covered with blood. The thugs left the house believing that the couple was dead.

Yet, brave neighbors risked their lives to help others. The Bindereifs, whose garden was adjacent to Dr. Picard's back entrance, had heard screams and feared the worst! As soon as the situation allowed, they saw what had happened and offered their help. And how the Picards needed it! The Nazis had turned off the water at the Picards' house—one of their common harassments to make it impossible for them to stay there. They also patrolled outside the house during the day, and nighttime was their only opportunity to eat. Until the worst was over, the Bindereifs brought their neighbors water and food night after night via their back entrance and thus saved their lives. Difficult and disquieting months followed.

It almost seemed as if Dr. Picard could not escape from Germany with his wife. Yet, quite unexpectedly, a ray of hope appeared. It was so unexpected that the Picards could not even say good-bye to their kind neighbors. During World War I, Dr. Julius Picard had volunteered as a medical officer in the German army and saved at that time the life of a soldier from the Stuttgart area who had been seriously wounded. This veteran had established contact in intricate ways with Gustav, Dr. Picard's oldest son, who was a medical officer under General Patton, and finally also with father Picard in Sontheim. He had already bought two airline tickets to the United States. However, they had to fly from Portugal because they could no longer leave Germany by air. Only Dr. Julius Picard himself knew the exact plan for how they could get to the United States via Stuttgart to Portugal and from there to the U.S. He could not even tell his wife, Gertrude, the name of their benefactor.

It was high time. It became harder and harder to emigrate. Already the "final solution of the Jewish question" cast a shadow with its collective transports to the extermination camps. On December 7, 1940, the Picards left Sontheim. Some time before that, their house on Lauffener Strasse had been confiscated and declared to be "Altersheim Sontheim" (Sontheim Old People's Home). It became a transit camp for Jews, who were transported shortly thereafter to the extermination camps.

Finally, the family was united again in the United States, where the parents lived with the younger son in Illinois. For Gertrude, only a few years remained in the newly found freedom. Her injuries from *Kristallnacht* and the continued humiliations had broken her strength. Soon after her emigration, she passed away. However, Dr. Julius Picard lived to be more than ninety years old. He benefited from his gift for languages, learning to speak English fluently in a short time, and became a U.S. citizen in 1947. Throughout his life, he did not tell anyone the name of his benefactor from the state of Württemberg!

Yet, with this incident we have gotten ahead of ourselves.

The Ziefles were glad that the Picards were able to leave Germany in time to save their lives. But they were also sad that Germany had lost two upright and devoted citizens. Other "enemies" of the Party were not so lucky. More and more people were arrested. To be caught criticizing the Party or listening to foreign radio broadcasts meant almost certain imprisonment or sometimes even death. Also, during the day, acts of violence became more and more frequent.

We ARE barbarians! We want to be KNOWN as barbarians!
—Adolf Hitler

four

September 1939

THE *Volksempfänger*, OR "People's Radio," crackled to life as the thumping beat of march music faded. "Achtung! Achtung! The German armed forces, the Wehrmacht, has repulsed Polish attacks on Germany's border. The armies of the Third Reich have now invaded Poland. We will not tolerate violations of our territory! Stay tuned for further developments. Heil Hitler!"

Pale and shaken, Georg Ziefle sat before the radio. Not wanting to hear more, he finally leaned forward and switched it off. Shaking his head from side to side, he murmured, "Germany is headed for her doom. I can feel it."

"Please, Papa!" Maria pleaded in a hoarse whisper. "The children." Maria raised her voice. "Reinhold, Kurt—tell me some more about your work in the harvest this summer."

Attempting to change the subject was useless; the boys were more interested in the war. Maria finally herded them outside to play.

But outside, the neighborhood was buzzing excitedly over the prospect of a new war. Powerless to protect her children from the winds of war, Maria watched anxiously as innocent minds were entranced by the romance of conflict without comprehending the bloodshed and destruction.

It was September 1, 1939. In Sontheim and throughout Germany, the Third Reich considered itself strong and invincible. Two days later, France and England declared war on Germany. The call to arms ensnared able-bodied men wherever the swastika cast its shadow. Maria Ziefle now faced the additional fear of a fatherless family. But the uncertainty did not last long; within a few days, Georg received orders to join the Wehrmacht.

That was too much for Maria. Until now, she could maintain the rigid exterior that had successfully protected her tender spirit. Yet, as she sat alone in the house nursing little Helmut, she wept silently—for her husband and her children, especially for this little one. And she prayed.

I do not understand why all of this is happening to us, but because You are God, I will trust You. Somehow, Lord, make a way for Georg not to have to fight, actually not to kill people! Yesterday, when he told the Wehrmacht officers that it was against his conscience to bear arms, I thanked You for such a bold husband. But I am really afraid, Lord, that maybe they will imprison him now. Whatever happens, take care of us, please.

Nervously, the family waited during the next days for the Wehrmacht's answer. And then on Friday the answer came finally. As Maria pulled the letters out of the mailbox and shuffled through them, she suddenly stopped, feeling weak. It was a letter from the draft board—she was going to lose her husband.

But she was mistaken. Her trembling fingers opened the envelope, and inside were orders for Georg to report to the *Sicherheits und Hilfsdienst* (the SHD, or Security and Emergency Service) that was also in charge of the four *Rettungsstellen*, also called Red Cross Stations or First-Aid Stations in Heilbronn. How nice it would be if he could be assigned after his training to *Rettungsstelle* I on Wilhelmstrasse, a little more than a mile from home.

Georg returned from work that day looking worn, his face reflecting frustration and worry. Maria called to him as she heard him climbing the stairs slowly. "Papa! We have good news! The draft board sent orders for you to report to the Security and Emergency Service." Georg's pace quickened miraculously, and he hurried into the kitchen where his wife stood. With a cautious smile, he asked, "Are you serious, Mama?"

"There's the letter on the table; read it for yourself."

He snatched up the letter and read it quickly, trembling. "It's true! I won't have to fight!" He put his arms around his wife exuberantly. "Our prayers are answered! God is still taking care of us!"

Maria nodded happily, her joy and relief evident in her smile.

&

Poland was now trampled by the German *blitzkrieg,* or lightning war, and most of the people of Sontheim, as across Germany, were ecstatic with their apparent invincibility. But Georg and Maria were not deceived. After all, why would more and more men have to be pressed into the Security and Emergency Service if Germany's armed forces were having overwhelming success? It made no sense to men who viewed the world with a sense of reason.

Georg's Security and Emergency Service duty began with several weeks of training, and allowed no visits at home. Maria was granted only one visit each week. Morale in the Ziefle home waned in spite of their happiness at Georg's duty without weapons. Maria was not only forced to shoulder all of the responsibilities of the household but also constantly had to bolster the children's spirits as they begged, "When will Papa finally come home?"

Georg appeared at home unexpectedly on a Sunday in mid-November. Maria was preparing lunch after church when she heard his footsteps coming up the stairs. She ran to greet him. "Georg! Why are you allowed to come home? And how thin you have become!"

"The food—it's been very hard on my stomach. I've been sick for several days, so Dr. Wagner gave me permission to eat at home from now on. And training is almost over, so soon I'll be off-duty every other day. I think your cooking will get me quickly back to full strength, Mama."

"I'm so glad, Georg! What would you like for lunch?"

"Just some gruel. That's all I can take right now."

The three older children came in from playing. "Papa!" they cried as they ran to embrace him. Surrounding him with their arms and happy chatter, they began probing about his activities, as well as reporting to him all of their recent accomplishments, of course.

When the encounter with the three oldest children had subsided, Georg stole into his bedroom to see his youngest son. Five weeks had passed since he had been with any of the children. The twilight of the room and the innocence of the sleeping baby soothed him.

How can there be such peace here in the midst of war and hate? he wondered. *Dear Heavenly Father, You have answered my prayers. Thank You for taking good care of my family.*

When he returned to the living room upstairs, Georg noticed Ruth slouched on the deacon's bench, dejectedly paging through one of her favorite books. Puzzled, he asked, "What's wrong, Ruth? You look as if your best friend just left you."

Young Maidens in a May 1 Labor Day Parade, 1934, Sontheim.

"When I was playing in the street this morning, Herr L___ stopped and yelled at me for not saying 'Heil Hitler' and saluting right. He said I'd go to prison if I continued to disobey him. He always stops and threatens me."

"Well, how do you salute him?" Georg inquired.

"I raise my hand as if I'm going to catch a fly on my face, then I drop it right away. Ever since I had to join the junior division of the Federation of Young Maidens (main division, *Bund Deutscher Mädel,* or BDM, and junior section, *Jungmädelgruppe,* or JM for girls ten to fourteen years old) this year, I've had to salute, even though I don't want to." Ruth's voice quivered as she began to whimper. "I'm so scared of Herr L___ that when I see him coming down the street I try to hide, but I hardly ever get away in time."

Georg put his arm around his daughter and led her into the dining room where his gruel was waiting. After bowing to pray for his meal, he began to eat, counseling Ruth between mouthfuls, "Ruth, I don't want you to worry about

Georg Ziefle in front of his ambulance.

going to prison. Your mother and I are here to protect you from that. Besides, they're more interested in arresting adults than nice young girls."

"But he's so mean to me. He grabs my arm so hard that it hurts, and he curses at me." She looked at her father through her tears.

"Listen, I'm proud of you. Do you know that? You are standing up for what's right, even when everyone else is giving in to the Nazi lies. I'm certain even God is proud of you!

"Herr L____ is a man we should feel sorry for and pray for. He gets drunk very often, and I'm sure he's very unhappy. Even though he is a Nazi official, I've heard that he can hardly read—you can do better than that. I think he doesn't really care as much about the Nazis as about himself. If the communists were in control, he would probably become a communist just as easily as he has become a Nazi."

Georg gathered the family at the table for a time of prayer. They prayed for Georg's health, for their own unity, for Pastor Brendle—and for Herr L___, Ruth's tormentor.

It was time for Georg to return to his military duty. At least from now on he could be home every other day and for all meals. After his training, he was indeed assigned to Red Cross Station I on Wilhelmstrasse. He was satisfied with his job. What an answer to prayer!

Dr. Hofherr, his superior, was impressed with his sense of responsibility and his honesty and treated him well. Georg became a medical orderly and an ambulance driver whose vehicle was capable of carrying up to six injured people. He gave his vehicle meticulous care, keeping it ready for use at all times.

❦

Winter that year was quiet for the Ziefles. Georg regained his health after he resumed eating Maria's carefully planned meals. The pressures of the Nazi presence had not subsided, to be sure, but the family was learning to live under the cloud of criticism and intimidation. Reinhold still refused steadfastly to participate in Hitler Youth meetings, and he and Ruth continued to attend Sunday services with their parents. Kurt, however, insisted on being faithful to his Hitler Youth activities. The initial headiness of the citizens after Poland's demolition had subsided, and the war now seemed to be a matter of necessary inconvenience. After all, the armies of the Third Reich would soon smother all

Georg (standing, far left) with his comrades from the Red Cross in Heilbronn.

of Europe, and then peace would be permanent. But life was not normal, by far. Many of the eligible men had been conscripted into service, leaving their families without fathers and husbands. The women of Sontheim did their best to cope without their husbands, but the struggle was very evident in their faces.

Life was hardest for those who refused to compromise their beliefs and co-operate with National Socialism. The psychological pressure was strong, and many times the faith of even the strong collapsed.

Although the Third Reich was continually touted as invincible, the Nazis began to show an increased concern for the safety of the citizens in the event of an air attack. Even at the beginning of the war, people were ordered to keep their houses blacked out after dark. Now, however, the government had initiated an extensive air-raid-shelter program.

By early 1940, the people of Sontheim were fully involved in developing shelters. To cooperate with the program, the Ziefles began removing all flammable materials from their attic to prevent fueling a fire if a bomb ever struck their home. As soon as the rooms were cleared of newspapers, books, and other flammable items, workers from the city hall sprayed the interiors of the attic and cellar with a fire-resistant solution. The authorized neighborhood air warden inspected the results and gave official approval, after which he provided a fire extinguisher and gas masks for the adults and children and told them to store the equipment in the cellar.

The Ziefles' cellar was well suited for an air-raid shelter. Although it lacked large emergency exits, its almost yard-thick sandstone walls and sandstone ceiling gave it a vaultlike quality. Georg and his sons set about to equip the refuge properly. First, they obtained concrete slabs, which they positioned over the cellar windows. Then they constructed a half-dozen bunk beds that they "upholstered" with straw mattresses and pillows.

"I sure hope we won't have to use this place," Kurt declared. "The smell would drive me insane." The briny sauerkraut, the vegetables and meat (they did not have a refrigerator at that time), and the Krauters' two wine barrels gave the cellar an atmosphere that sent even the stouthearted reeling.

"If bombs are falling all around," Reinhold replied, "you will have altogether different worries!"

Kurt stiffened and answered resolutely, "The enemy planes will never be allowed to enter Germany. Our armies will take care of that!"

"I hope you're right," his father said quietly.

However, English scout planes soon began to fly over the Heilbronn area. The city held a large railroad center and considerable manufacturing; it was a likely target for an enemy bent on crippling a nation. Antiaircraft guns had been used several times to repel the planes, but because the aircraft kept at such a high altitude, such weapons had little effect. The local citizens were becoming increasingly concerned with the possibility of their community's being a military target without protection.

In addition to converting private cellars for shelters, the Nazis began to construct large public facilities for those who had no cellars or for those who were caught too far from their houses during an air attack. Commercial wine cellars were commandeered for this purpose. One air-raid shelter near the Matthäuskirche could hold more than two thousand people.

By July 1940, the air battles over England were in full fury. Newspaper and radio broadcasts were predicting repeatedly a quick victory.

One warm evening as Georg turned off the radio, he commented to Maria, "This seems so strange to me. If the war is going to be won so soon, why are the Nazis building all these air-raid shelters? They're working so furiously to have enough capacity; and, in their hurry, they're building shelters that I don't think are strong enough to withstand heavy bombing. That new one we pass on the way to church has both entrances so close together that one bomb could trap all the occupants. It looks to me as if we're facing the prospect of a long war."

"I expect you're right," Maria replied, sounding worried. "If that happens, what about our boys? It won't be long before they will be eligible for the draft. If they are taken into the service, what will happen to them—especially Kurt? We can help anchor their souls when they are here, but what can we do when they are in an army camp far away?"

Just then there was a knock at the door. Georg hurried to answer. As he opened the door, he was addressed with a stiff, "Heil Hitler!"

"Oh, it is you, Herr W___," Georg answered flatly.

"Herr Ziefle, I must speak with you and your wife immediately." His voice was cold.

"Why—certainly. Come in." Georg led him to the living room. He wondered about the nature of the visit. *W___, as the highest ranking Nazi in the neighborhood, may have something important and perhaps serious on his mind because of his stature and influence in the Party. I know that the Nazis have not been very happy with us because of our adherence to our Christian faith and lack of cooperation with their cause.*

"Heil Hitler, Frau Ziefle," he greeted as he approached Maria, who was seated on the couch. "We are disturbed that the two of you do not involve yourselves in our Nazi cause. We know that you do not contribute money, but we are even more concerned that you do not attend any of our meetings. I realize, Herr Ziefle, that your duties at the Red Cross station prevent you from attendance. However, your wife has proven her disrespect for the Party by not attending at all the meetings of the *Frauenschaft*, the Nazi Women's Organization, so the Party demands an explanation. You have two weeks to present your case to the committee. Use your time well. I will return after this deadline."

W___ whirled and disappeared through the door. Georg and Maria looked at each other in silent bewilderment as they listened to the man's boots clomp heavily down the stairs.

Maria grasped her husband's hand and pulled him down next to her. Biting her lip, she shook her head slowly. "Papa, I could go to prison for this—or be publicly humiliated."

Hitler Youth in a May 1 Labor Day Parade, 1934, Sontheim.

"Not as long as I'm alive," Georg assured her steadily. He took both of her hands in his. They sat silently, each mentally presenting their dilemma to God.

"I think the Lord has given me an idea," Georg exclaimed suddenly, giving his wife's hands a squeeze. "You've been having problems with phlebitis for all these years, and since Helmut's birth, it's been worse. Maybe if Dr. Wagner examined you, he could verify that you are physically unable to attend the meetings. Then the Nazis would leave you alone!"

Three days later, Dr. Wagner examined Maria and recommended in his medical certificate that she be excused from meetings for health reasons. His advice was accepted, and Maria was no longer troubled regarding the meetings.

German optimism waxed strong as Nazi forces swept across Denmark and Norway on the north and France on the west. Encouraged by Hitler's victories, Mussolini also declared war on the Allies. As the German victories mounted, Maria noticed that neighbors who had been lukewarm or indifferent toward Hitler began to increase in apparent loyalty and fervor for the Führer.

The Nazis were no longer persecuting only Jews and staunch Christians but anyone who refused to accept the *Deutschglaube,* or the German way of life, as the only and ultimate religion. *Deutschglaube* had its roots in two-thousand-year-old Germanic folklore that glorified national heroism, purity of race, and German destiny to rule the world. Anyone who deviated from these Nazi ideals was either reeducated, harassed, imprisoned, or sometimes even exiled or murdered.

The Nazis exhibited little respect for an individual's ability, experience, or character as they appointed people to positions of leadership in government and business. Party loyalty was all that mattered. Only thus was it possible that men such as the alcoholic Herr L___ were prime candidates for leadership in those days.

Maria considered these matters as she sat in front of her house and watched the children play with Helmut. What could a parent do to instill in one's children values of decency, respect, faithfulness, and diligence when all around the only thing that seemed to guarantee success was the rejection of such qualities? She presented her frustrations to her God.

I have no doubt, Lord, that Your grace is sufficient. But I doubt myself. Is my faith sufficient to endure these times?

In the midst of social turmoil and the tension of war, Maria had to laugh as she watched Kurt whirl Helmut about their small yard in the battered stroller. There was still happiness in their midst; love and innocence still survived under Maria and Georg's strong determination. But how long would it last? The swastika never retreated; rather, it made itself increasingly more evident as it laid siege against the Ziefle household.

By God's mercy, I have not lost my husband to the war, but what about Reinhold and Kurt? What about the demands for conformity upon Ruth? And will Helmut enter manhood knowing only war cries and persecution?

Life would never be as it was, but how Maria longed to return to the times of peace.

She reflected back to what seemed like years ago, to the moments right after the appalling announcement that Germany had invaded Poland. As Maria had attempted to divert the children's attention from the gruesome subject, Reinhold, his young face filled with bewilderment, had asked, "Papa, what is war?"

Kurt enjoys taking his little brother, Helmut, for a ride in his baby carriage in our neighborhood on Ackermannstrasse.

Helmut enjoys the outdoors in his stroller.

It is grace, nothing but grace that today we can still live in the fellowship (communion) of Christian sisters and brothers.

—Dietrich Bonhoeffer

five

Autumn 1941

THE WAR CONTINUED TO ESCALATE. Germany had already been fighting with Russia for several months, and rumors hinted of future conflict with the United States. The radio announcers continually glorified German victories on all fronts.

And in Sontheim itself the war also was edging closer. Several times during the summer, air-raid sirens had sounded an early warning with two short blasts—enemy planes had been sighted flying toward unknown targets in southern Germany.

✦

It was on a late Sunday night in mid-October when Maria, alone in bed, was again awakened by two short warning blasts. She stumbled across the dark room, found her robe, and slipped it on. Hurrying up the stairs to the attic, she called, "Reinhold! Kurt! To the cellar!"

Kurt sleepily answered, "Mama, we're not afraid. Nothing has happened to Sontheim yet. Please let us stay in bed."

Reluctantly, Maria gave in. "Just make sure that if you hear the full alarm—or planes—you'll come to the cellar immediately."

"Yes, Mama."

She went quickly downstairs, woke Ruth, and picked up two-and-a-half-year-old Helmut from his bed. By candlelight, the three nervously descended to the cellar and tried to make themselves comfortable on the straw mattresses. Ruth and Helmut quickly fell asleep, but their mother lay tensely in the dark, pungent dampness. Their neighbors, the Krauters, had not come down either; Maria surmised that they also were ignoring the sirens.

An hour passed in silence. Then two hours. It was now after midnight. Suddenly, the sirens came to life. Would it be the long all clear or the minute-long blasts of the full alarm? Maria, poised to run for her sons, listened as the first wailing blast began to die and a second began. She leaped from the bunk and shook Ruth. "Watch Helmut. I'm going to get the boys!"

As she reached the cellar door, a deafening explosion made the house shudder. Maria, her heart pounding, rushed up the stairway screaming, "Reinhold! Kurt!"

"We're coming! We're coming!" Sleep having gone as quickly as the explosion, the frantic teenagers scurried down, their bare feet slapping on the wooden steps. They rushed breathlessly through the door, and Maria closed the latch behind them. Shivering in their pajamas, the boys listened to a strange new sound—the eerie whistling of a descending bomb, then another thudding explosion.

"Boys," Maria spoke sternly, "the next time you hear a warning siren, you will immediately come to the cellar. Is that clear?"

Their mother's instructions had never been so clear. They replied sheepishly, "Yes, Mama, we will."

"Children, we must pray for your father. He may be busy tonight, and work could be very dangerous." They all knelt down next to the bunks.

Even Helmut lisped his simple request, "God, take care of Papa."

The explosions stopped after only a few minutes as suddenly as they had begun. The silence seemed almost as threatening as the explosions. Finally, the all-clear sirens began their wail—a long, sustained blast. Maria led her little family back to their rooms.

In a few minutes, Maria lay under her covers, trying vainly to ease the tension in her body. She chuckled nervously as she recalled the frequently broadcast statement by Hermann Göring, supreme commander of the Luftwaffe: "My name is nothing if even one enemy plane crosses the German border."

The next morning, after Georg returned safely for breakfast, the family went

Air-raid shelter in Heilbronn during World War II.

to survey the damage. The first hit had been only a half-mile from their house; an incendiary bomb had devastated a private home. Reinhold, awed by the smoldering wreckage, murmured, "If that had hit our house, Kurt, you and I would both be dead. I'll never ignore another siren."

The Heilbronn area was attacked again after seven weeks, but damage was relatively light. The citizens comforted themselves with the possibility that the enemy was losing its potency and soon their worries would be over. But four days later, Germany declared war on the United States—a strange, faraway enemy with a huge country and almost unlimited resources. The rhetoric of optimism was ringing very hollow indeed.

But it was not the bombs and the realities of war that taxed one's endurance. It was the strain of coping in the midst of an oppressive society. Good friends now eyed each other with suspicion. Kindness was an act of weakness. Loyalty to conscience was treason. Most of the Ziefles had already entrenched themselves against this onslaught of evil, of moral decay. And they had sadly, with great concern, watched Kurt and his enthusiasm for the new order. But now it was beginning to wear thin for him too. The warmth of love in his home had kept something alive inside him. And it wasn't just the matter of the Jews. He was only fourteen, and already pressures that could crack a man were closing in on him.

Recognizing his physical prowess and his sharp mind, the Hitler Youth directors had appointed Kurt to a chief squad leader in his group. In athletic competition, Kurt was always one of the winners, and when they played war games that served as premilitary training, his group would rally under his natural leadership abilities and defeat their competitors. The weekly meetings of the Hitler Youth were two- and three-hour yelling sessions. They were kept at a high emotional pitch with songs and loud exhortations on excellence while the boys stood rigidly at attention or goose-stepped like storm troopers for an hour at a time.

The pressure to succeed drained Kurt. He was no longer able to attend school, for he had taken a man's job. So much manpower had been diverted to the war that businesses began drawing personnel from those below draft age. Kurt was hired as a clerk at the *Kreissparkasse,* the district's savings bank, in Heilbronn. Right away on the first day, he, like everyone else who worked in such institutions, had to swear an oath to Adolf Hitler before the Nazi district leader. The job was exciting at first, but the workload and responsibilities began to increase.

In addition to the pressures of his work there, his troubles were compounded by some of the young women employees. Several of them had begun making romantic advances toward him and, at his young age, Kurt was confused and frustrated further.

Inside, he was in turmoil. The Nazis had fostered too much pride in his soul for him to admit his troubles to his parents. He had nowhere to turn. In addition, Kurt had once participated in a Protestant youth meeting in Waiblingen when a large piece of iron came flying from the outside through the stained glass window of the church. Fortunately, no one was hurt by this incident.

However, this experience made a lasting impression on him. He despised such violence by the Nazi Party. He finally reached the breaking point on New Year's Day, 1942, just a few days before his fifteenth birthday. Kurt had worked all day and into the night figuring interest rates. He came home, and after a few hours of troubled sleep, he left the house quietly with a small bag of clothes under his arm. With a sense of desperation, he rode the streetcar to the train station. Pretending to be on bank business, he purchased a ticket to Stuttgart. From there, he made connections to Friedrichshafen, Innsbruck, and finally to Feldkirch, a little Austrian village on the Swiss border. There, a tall barbed-wire fence stood between him and freedom.

Unsure as to how to cross the border and without money to rent a room, he slept for two nights in restaurants while trying to formulate a plan. Unfortunately, he had been reported to the border patrol as a suspicious person, and on the third day he was picked up by the police.

A policemen checked his identification and made a call to Sontheim. Kurt was arrested as a deserter and escorted back to his hometown. Georg and Maria, in great distress over their son's disappearance, had called the bank and many of his friends but had received no clues as to his whereabouts. When the authorities called and told them to take their son home, they were greatly relieved. But for many weeks, Kurt remained silent about his attempted escape; he was still too proud to admit weakness.

To Kurt's and the family's amazement, the Hitler Youth leaders did not discipline him. Herr H___, his local leader in the Hitler Youth (who, having the rank of *Gefolgschaftsführer,* was in charge of about 90 boys in Sontheim; normally a *Gefolgschaftsführer* would be in charge of about 150 boys, but Sontheim was a smaller town), lied about the incident and told everyone that Kurt had attempted to join the army in Italy. He even arranged for him to attend a ski course, which was reserved exclusively for soldiers. Upon returning, Kurt was restored again to Chief Squad Leader directly under H___. The Nazis knew how important good leaders were. Although Kurt was the youngest member in the group, his physical strength and reputation gained him much respect from his fellow Hitler Youth.

With Kurt in the forefront, Reinhold's absence from the meetings was increasingly obvious. At school and on the street, his friends and the Hitler Youth leaders continually hounded him about the matter. Kurt made clear to his brother that he could get into serious difficulties if he continued to skip the

Hitler Youth meetings. Because Kurt was responsible for checking the attendance at the Hitler Youth meetings in Sontheim, he helped his brother by not marking him absent. However, he could not do so indefinitely. Similarly, he also helped young Catholic men who were not in attendance and excused them so that they would not get into trouble. In April, Reinhold finally gave in.

At his first meeting, the boys stood at attention during the roll call. Suddenly H___ screamed, "Reinhold Ziefle! Why has it taken you so long to show up for the Hitler Youth meetings? You were ordered to do so a year ago!"

Reinhold, intimidated by the shouting and by the forty-five Hitler Youth staring at him, remained silent. H___ stormed toward him furiously, his fist raised to strike Reinhold's face. The gymnasium was silent. The man stood before Reinhold, seething, his fist still poised. The boys waited eagerly to see what their leader would do. Reinhold lifted his arm to protect himself.

H___ realized that he was no match for the muscular boy and that Kurt would no doubt leap to his brother's defense. Humiliated, the leader stepped back and resumed the roll call.

Eager for revenge, H___ reported Reinhold's delinquency to the *Stammführer* (Regional Leader in charge of six hundred boys), and Reinhold was quickly demoted to the closely watched Compulsory Hitler Youth. Most of the boys there were half-Jews and did their training under police surveillance. They were treated as second-class citizens, and Reinhold became increasingly embittered against the Nazis.

In that same month in 1942, Reinhold, by then almost seventeen, completed his junior high school studies and became a commercial apprentice in a small dry-goods store in Heilbronn. Wilhelm Sch___, the proprietor, made little effort to teach him how to manage the store, so Reinhold spent most days performing only odd tasks.

But Reinhold was fascinated with truth. He was not afraid to defy the Nazis, and he began making every effort to discover what was really occurring in the world. The Nazis censored all information that came in the newspapers and on the radio; so, to satisfy his hunger, Reinhold began secretly to modify the family's *Volksempfänger* to receive shortwave broadcasts from England. Listening to such broadcasts was, of course, illegal, so he also set about building earphones from materials he could salvage.

He finally completed his project at the end of April. After midnight, he would test the unit in the attic bedroom he shared with Kurt. He waited eagerly in his bed one night until he heard the 12:30 chimes of the clock in the living room below. He rose silently to his feet and picked up the radio that was hidden in a box. Seated in the darkness as far from Kurt as possible, Reinhold plugged the unit into the wall socket and switched it on, pulling the headphones over his ears.

Static carried across the room, and then the faraway sound of a voice. Kurt began to stir, and finally sat up, vainly blinking in an attempt to see through the blackness. "What are you doing? Why are you listening to the radio in the middle of the night?" he muttered.

Reinhold, overjoyed with his success, whispered incautiously, "Quiet, I'm getting a broadcast from England!"

"Are you crazy?" Kurt jumped out of bed. "Don't you know you could end up in jail for this?"

"I don't care. I'm tired of constantly hearing lies about victory. I'm going to find the truth, even if the Nazis kill me! I want freedom like they have in the West."

"I could never do what you're doing," Kurt said thoughtfully. "But I promise I won't betray you—you're my brother, after all. Please be careful, though! The Nazis would be more than happy to shoot you—if you're caught."

Reinhold listened a while longer, then pulled the headphones from his head and switched off the radio. "Poor signal tonight. Maybe it won't fade out so much tomorrow." He felt his way back to the bed and began to crawl in.

"Kurt, I appreciate your keeping this a secret. You're a great brother."

Kurt, already falling asleep, grunted acknowledgment. Reinhold lay tingling with the thrill of success. Now he would know the truth. The clock below chimed once.

❧

The warm winds of spring were beginning to soften the countryside with new life now. Gardens and fields were green again, and the hedges and colorful flowers fascinated Helmut, who had just turned three. He was now old enough to appreciate the beauty around him but, fortunately, unable to comprehend the miseries of war and the brutalities of the Nazis.

But 1942 was the quietest year of the war for the Ziefles, despite its traumatic beginning when Kurt tried to flee the country. Although life was becoming harsher, both physically and socially, the pressures seemed to escalate more slowly. Air raids were almost nonexistent, except for one in early May, when seven people in the area were killed.

For the children, one of the hardest situations with which to cope at this time was the mounting scarcity of nonessential food items. Most such items were either diverted to the fighting fronts or else stockpiled by the Nazi leaders for their own use. Although staples also were in short supply, the children had the most difficulty adjusting to the lack of chocolate and other candies that formerly filled rows of glass jars in the stores with color and aroma.

For the Ziefle children, there was one small box of hard candies, which Maria guarded for special use on birthdays, Christmas, and Easter. Two days after Christmas, Helmut approached her with a forlorn expression, "Mama, can't we have some more candy on New Year's Day?"

It was hard for Maria to refuse such a plaintive request. "I'm sorry, Helmut, but you'll have to wait about three more months until your birthday. Then you can choose two more candies from the box."

"Is that a long time, Mama?"

She smiled at his innocence. "It is for a three-year-old boy. But you'll just have to be patient." Even the children's candy was not immune from the shadow of Hitler's regime.

Before long, the inconveniences broadened to include far more essential commodities. As the war effort heightened, the government confiscated the Ziefles' automobile. Private citizens were no longer allowed to own cars. The Ziefles' BMW was turned over to a doctor.

As Reinhold continued to listen surreptitiously to the news from England, he became firmly convinced that Germany faced certain defeat against the superior resources of the Allies. Nearly eighteen now, he was very concerned about being drafted into the German armed forces. After Christmas, he admitted his fears to Kurt. "What will happen to me if I'm drafted? You're a Chief Squad Leader in the Hitler Youth, but what about me? I don't even know how to handle a gun, let alone hit a target. Can you point out to me at least a couple of things?"

Kurt was glad to assist his brother and began to teach him basic military skills. Neither of them knew how timely this decision was. Although Reinhold was still only seventeen, two weeks later an envelope from the draft board appeared in the mail addressed to him. He opened it slowly, finally pulling out the letter. The entire family was silently standing around him as he scanned the message quickly.

Dejected, he looked up. "I'm to report to Hitler's *Reichsarbeitsdienst,* the labor service, in Renchen near Achern, on Tuesday, January 13, 1943. Every young German between the ages of eighteen and twenty-five has to serve six months for premilitary training." Renchen is located in the Rhine valley close to the foothills of the Black Forest. Reinhold looked at his family, groping for words to express his feelings, "Now—now I won't be able to complete my apprenticeship."

No one was more disappointed over Reinhold's induction than his mother. Even at the initial announcement, her eyes became moist. She said as little as possible, even to Georg; but on the long nights when he was on duty, she would lie on her bed and weep silently at the thought of losing her firstborn— putting his life in the custody of a government that had no respect for life or its Creator.

Dämmerstündle on the evening of January 12 was a somber event. The possibility that this could be their final time together as a family was obvious to all of them. They knelt in a circle about Reinhold and committed him to God's keeping. Even Kurt could not restrain tears that night. And three-year-old Helmut, sensing in his spirit what his mind did not comprehend, gave Reinhold an extra-long hug.

The next morning, Maria, Kurt, Ruth, and Helmut walked soberly with Reinhold toward the Staufenbergstrasse streetcar stop. Georg had already said his good-bye, unable to get time off from his job.

Inwardly, Maria cried for strength, but she did her best to make the farewell as pleasant as possible. She held Reinhold's arm tightly. "Son, remain strong in your faith. You know that God is everywhere, and He will be with you." She hesitated as she strained to stifle her emotions. "Even though I can't be with you, my prayers and all that I've taught you—"

"Mama, please don't worry about me. I can face today because God gives me strength—and I'll always depend on Him. He will take good care of me— right, Mama?"

Maria forced a tearful smile and squeezed his arm. "I'm proud of you; and God will keep you. I'm sure He will." She wasn't nearly as certain in her heart. She had no doubts about God's role, but the pressures on Reinhold would be so great.

The streetcar came clanking down the street, and the sad party hurried toward the stop. They all wrapped their arms about him together. As the others stepped back, Maria held him close and kissed him. The tears on their cheeks mixed together. Reluctantly, she dropped her arms, and Reinhold stepped briskly toward the car, clutching his bag.

The four on the street watched silently as Reinhold paid his fare and hurried to a seat next to a curb-side window. With loud creaks and groans, the streetcar began to roll away. Reinhold lifted his hand and smiled sadly at his family. His loved ones waved slowly as their son and brother disappeared down the street. The wind was cold.

During the next days, Maria could hardly restore her normal routine. She was constantly filled with thoughts and prayers for her absent son.

After two-and-a-half weeks, a letter arrived. Georg, off-duty that day, brought the unopened letter quickly in to Maria.

Dear Father and Mother:

I have been assigned to the mortar division of the *Waffen-SS* and will be leaving from Renchen to Unna near Dortmund on Monday, February 1 for basic training in warfare. When you receive this I will probably have only a few days left to stay here. I wish I could see you before I have to leave.

Love,
Reinhold

As Maria read the letter, she felt dizzy; her worst fears had come to pass. She handed it silently to Georg.

As he read, his face became flushed, and his jaws tightened. "They can't do this! Don't they know Reinhold isn't even eighteen yet?" He stopped for a moment to gather his thoughts. The *Waffen-SS* (Armed SS) was the military formation of the *Allgemeine-SS* (General SS) in which they indoctrinated and trained elite troops for active duty on war fronts. They had very dangerous assignments. "I don't want my son in that outfit," Georg declared.

"But what can we do?" Maria asked.

"We will go to Stuttgart today and speak with the people who are responsible. If we catch the next train, we should be able to reach the regional head-quarters of the SS before four o'clock."

The children were home from school that day, and when Kurt heard of Reinhold's assignment, he seemed almost as upset as his parents. It did not seem fair that Reinhold, who had no sympathy for the Nazi cause, should have to risk his life to such a degree in its defense.

"Don't worry," Kurt assured his parents. "Ruth and I will take care of Helmut. And I'll call Papa's Red Cross Station and tell them where he is."

"Thank you, son," Maria replied as she and Georg prepared quickly for the trip. "Please pray for us too."

As the couple sat in the train, gazing at the countryside, Maria turned to her husband and said, "I feel as if we're walking right into the lions' den. I wonder how Daniel felt?" Georg smiled stiffly as she continued, "I don't think we've ever faced anything this difficult together, have we?"

Georg sat with his hands folded on his lap. "I'm afraid that the lions we're going to face are quite hungry."

The train slowed as it neared the outskirts of Stuttgart. Maria's heart began to beat heavily and her palms felt moist and cold. She looked at Georg's eyes; as a salesman, he knew how to look confident, but his eyes could not conceal his apprehension. He nervously glanced at his watch, his thoughts and prayer a jumble in his mind.

If I did not love my son so much, Lord, I wouldn't even dare to do this. I'll probably look back on this time and think I was crazy. But I don't want Reinhold to go to the Waffen-SS; I don't want to lose him. You are God, and I'm just a little speck on the earth—yet You care about us and about Reinhold. But if he must go to war, go with him and keep his faith strong. We may lose our son, but I don't want You to lose his soul.

To their relief, the Ziefles had only a short walk from the train station to the regional SS headquarters. As they neared the doors, Georg glanced again at his watch—almost four o'clock. Inside, they approached a sergeant seated at a desk. "Sir, we would like to see the *Untersturmführer,* the Second Lieutenant, concerning our son, who is stationed at Renchen."

He took their names, then rose and approached an officer at the back of the room. They spoke quietly. The *Hauptscharführer,* or master sergeant, walked briskly back, sat down at his desk, and without looking up said flatly, "You may see him at five o'clock."

Georg thanked him and joined Maria on a wooden bench to wait. After sitting still as long as he could, Georg finally stood and paced the floor quietly. Maria stared at her feet, gripping her gloves tightly.

Just after five, two guards approached them and escorted them into the Second Lieutenant's office. The man made a few quick notes on a pad of paper, then peered at the couple. Benevolence was nowhere on his countenance. "Are you Ziefle?" he barked.

"Yes, sir."

"Whatever you want, get to the point. My time is too valuable for chitchat."

"Sir, first I thank you for giving us your time." Georg spoke gently but confidently. "My son, Reinhold, is being drafted into the *Waffen-SS* without my knowledge or permission. He's only seventeen, so he has no business being sent to the fighting front. I request that you release him from the *Waffen-SS*."

The officer leaped from his chair, slamming his fist on the desk as he rose. "Are you an idiot?" he shouted. "Do you know what you're asking me to do?"

Maria held Georg's arms tightly, trying to keep him calm. Georg remained in control of his emotions as he answered, "We're concerned only about our son. He's not even of age yet, and he still needs us."

The officer glared at the couple and growled, "I should have both of you arrested for this act of treason! What do you think would happen to our national defense if we allowed every soldier to go wherever his mama or papa wanted him, eh? The only way you could possibly have him released is to see Himmler personally."

Himmler, head of the SS, had terrorized Germany. To approach him with such a request would be totally absurd and life threatening.

Maria's heart sank in despair. She could feel Georg droop slightly. Her eyes already flooding with tears, she timidly asked, "May we see Reinhold while he is in Renchen, before he is transferred?"

"The standard visitation time is thirty minutes. You may see him in the morning. Now get going. I have others waiting to see me yet this afternoon."

The couple, hanging their heads, walked out the door and through the main office. Maria pressed her gloves tightly against her mouth to muffle her sobs. Georg gently put his arm around her and led her toward the train station. The twilight kindly hid their misery from curious eyes. The train ride home seemed twice as long.

The next morning, Georg and Maria drove to the military camp at Renchen.

Reinhold Ziefle.

Georg had received permission to borrow a Red Cross car for the trip. The reunion was not what they had hoped for. They had no privacy, but sat with Reinhold in a large hall bustling with trainees and officers. It was almost impossible to express private thoughts.

Reinhold was as disappointed as his parents about their failure to gain his release, but he tried to accept the inevitable with stoicism.

As their half-hour drew to a close, the three sat stiffly in their chairs, glancing at one another uncomfortably. Maria, unable to hold back, finally burst out weeping and bent forward to hold her son in her arms. Georg and his son stared at each other through the tears that were welling up in their eyes.

Reinhold spoke, his voice trembling. "Mama, Papa, I will miss you—and I love both of you, and Kurt and Ruth and Helmut too." He stopped to gather his emotions. "Tell them how much I miss them, please?"

Maria and Georg nodded, neither of them trusting their voices.

Reinhold tried his best to smile as he assured them, "Don't worry; everything will be all right. God will take care of us. True?"

Georg cast aside his self-consciousness and put both arms around his firstborn. "God be with you, Reinhold." He turned his head to hide the streams of tears. An officer was approaching to announce the end of their half-hour. Georg took his wife's arm and pulled her up gently from her chair. "We must go." The two slowly moved toward the door, trying to maintain composure. As Georg pushed the door open, they looked back once more. Reinhold, in his uniform, lifted his hand timidly. His jaw trembling, he whirled and walked the other way.

From Unna near Dortmund, Reinhold was transferred via Holland and Belgium to Southern France, where he was trained in the Pyrenees in mortar warfare. His company belonged to the division *Frundsberg*. Fortunately, both he and his immediate superior, the *Zugführer*, a twenty-year-old platoon leader, took a liking to each other, and that made life easier for Reinhold. However, his young superior was soon transferred because he was promoted to the rank of *Obersturmführer*, or first lieutenant, and received his own company command.

When Reinhold was transferred to Bordeaux in 1943, without this platoon leader and was stationed there in barracks, his situation deteriorated. He felt lonely because as a believing Christian his comrades did not understand him and he could not engage in their loose, disorderly way of life. They asked him to come along when they visited immoral girls, but he declined. In his frustration, he wrote to his parents that he could not find one comrade in his unit who believed in Jesus and with whom he could have devotions. This letter was intercepted and opened by the military censors. The next day, Reinhold had to line up in front of his entire company, and the company commander bawled him out thoroughly. He thundered that it was a great crime for an SS man to have such thoughts because Jesus had also been a Jew. After he had scolded Reinhold in front of the unit, he had to do punishment drills. Both the company leader, the *Kompanieführer,* and the new platoon leader, the *Zugführer,* both of whom had been well disposed toward Reinhold before, had now withdrawn their favor.

As a demotion, Reinhold was then assigned to the company *Regiment des Führers,* which belonged to the division *Das Reich* on the eastern front. That reassignment almost certainly saved Reinhold's life. In the middle of January, he was wounded in Shitomir near Kiev. A bullet from a Russian machine gun fired at a distance of three hundred to four hundred meters lodged in his body. Because of the great distance, the bullet did not kill him, but it got stuck in the

Ziefle family, in war year 1944, with Helmut on bottom left.

back muscles in front of his lungs. He was taken right away to a hospital in Marienbad near Czechoslovakia not so much because of his wound but because of dysentery. He had blood in his bowel movements, and nothing stayed in his body. He informed his parents about his condition, and Kurt visited him at the end of January in 1944. This meeting gave the two brothers a rare opportunity to see each other again, exchange experiences, and encourage one another.

Reinhold's understanding doctor treated his wound only superficially because he did not want to send him back to the Russian front. He let the wound continue to discharge to save him from an almost certain death on the eastern front. One had very few chances of survival there. The doctor had to be careful so that his protracted method of treatment did not raise suspicion.

Toward the end of February, Reinhold was able to come home for three days, and the bullet was removed on March 20 with the help of a magnet. The Ziefles stored it for a long time in their china cabinet as proof of God's protection in Reinhold's life.

At the end of March, Reinhold was released from the hospital and was given fourteen days convalescent leave and fourteen days home leave. For him, it was a welcome break from the insecurity and danger at the front. During this time, he built a small bunker in the allotment garden as an emergency cover and shelter during air-raids. This was very important because the garden was almost one kilometer away from home.

At the beginning of May, he was transferred for recovery to the convalescent company in the Heinrich-Himmler-Barracks to Prague and at the end of May to the junior leadership school in The Hague, Holland. His training was brief because he was on a lot of guard duty because of the impending danger of an invasion, especially after D-Day, June 6, 1944, in Normandy.

After The Hague, Reinhold saw action in Arnheim, where he guarded and looked after more than one hundred fifty American prisoners of war in a POW camp. At times, he also had to do guard duty at the important Rhine Bridge at Arnheim. In December, the Allies launched a great air attack on that bridge. Yet, at the end of November, Reinhold was assigned again to his old division *Frundsberg* for replacement. Meanwhile, Reinhold's blond comrade with whom he had been trained in the division *Frundsberg* had been promoted from *Granatwerfer,* or mortar commander, to *Zugführer,* or platoon commander. Reinhold was assigned to this platoon. His old comrade told him that the com-

Ziefle family near footbridge across the Neckar River during Reinhold's leave in 1944.

pany in which Reinhold had served earlier had been almost totally wiped out during the D-Day invasion in Normandy. At the most, only two or three of his comrades had escaped. Upon receiving this news, Reinhold thanked God that He had saved his life at that time by means of a censored letter.

Revenge is a judgment, which is enjoyed coldly. We know exactly when England will be smashed. Then England will collapse. We will beat it into submission, and to be sure, day after day and night after night.
—Joseph Goebbels

six

September 1944

LIFE WAS NO LONGER PREDICTABLE. It almost was safer now to measure time in days, and no longer in months or even years. To survive and exist were honorable enough.

Now, even the basic food items—flour, sugar, meat, and milk—were in short supply, if they were available at all. The milk was so watered down it was blue. The Ziefles focused their energies on finding enough to eat. Georg repaired a farmer's sewing machine in exchange for food. At harvest time, Maria and the children gleaned the fields and were glad for every ear of grain they found to supplement their meager food supply. They often had to walk a long way to find a field that had not yet been picked clean by other families. The work was slow and tiring and, for a five-year-old like Helmut, the days never went fast enough. But hungry stomachs provided all of the incentive needed when there was no food at home.

Ingenuity was in demand. To make syrup that she could substitute for sugar, Maria simmered a kettle full of sugar beets for a week. To ensure that they had eggs and meat, the Ziefles kept a dozen hens in the shed adjoining their house, and several rabbits in cages behind the house. Ruth had her pets, although now she kept them for reasons other than companionship!

Because the Nazis had supported having large families, the Ziefles had been rewarded with the already mentioned allotment garden, a moderate-sized garden plot about fifteen minutes on foot from their home. They wasted nothing from the garden. They fed the greens from the vegetables to the rabbits. That was not enough, however, so Maria often sent Helmut to pick grass along roads and ditches as supplemental feed for the creatures.

There was no way of avoiding the preoccupation with finding food; sometimes even Maria had the sensation that she was living an animal existence, merely trying to survive from one meal to another.

But soon they were to be tested by a new threat. September was almost over. Ruth, busy with studies from her new school in Heilbronn, was specializing in chemistry. Helmut, when he wasn't hungry, was occupied with his playmates. Kurt had been accepted by the German Air Force after he had passed the first flying tests in gliding and was waiting eagerly to report that week to flight training school at Dettingen, Teck. He had completed Hitler's Labor Service in Brünn, Czechoslovakia, from May to July.

One event had touched him very much during that time. He shared his room in the barracks with several comrades. One of them was the son of Baron von Rassler, the general of air defense. He came from Constance at Lake Constance and had his bunk on the right side from Kurt's. Often, Kurt had conversations with him and knew his point of view. It was the same as his; both of them loved Germany but not the Nazis. One or two days before the attempt on Hitler's life on July 20, 1944, this general visited his son in the barracks. Kurt, too, had seen him. This was the only visit of the general; furthermore, for someone with such a high rank to visit a National Labor Service Camp was quite unusual. Perhaps von Rassler spoke with his son about the planned attempt on Hitler's life on July 20. He was closely related to Claus Schenk Graf von Stauffenberg, who was executed on July 20, 1944, after his attempt on Hitler's life; his wife was a member of the von Stauffenberg family. For Kurt, having the chance to get to know this young man and thus to establish a personal connection to these dramatic historic events was something special.

It was Wednesday night, and Georg wanted to discuss the future with Kurt. "I suppose you have much to do if you'll be leaving for training on Saturday," he began.

Kurt was studying the instruction sheet that came with his acceptance to the Air Force.

"Not really, Papa. About all I have left is to say good-bye to my friends."

Kurt Ziefle as recruit of the Luftwaffe (German Air Force).

Maria interrupted as she glanced up from her needlework, "This house will be so empty with both you and Reinhold gone."

Georg gazed at Kurt seriously. "I am so glad that you do not have to go to the Waffen-SS like Reinhold. But flying—especially in war—is terribly dangerous. Are you really sure that is what you want to do?"

Kurt grinned confidently and leaned back in the sofa. "Oh, Papa, you worry too—"

A horrible explosion shattered the peacefulness and rattled the windows. As if by reflex, Georg shouted, "To the cellar! I'll get Helmut from the bedroom!" The three were already rushing down the stairs. Georg dashed into the bedroom to retrieve Helmut. The two arrived in the cellar only seconds behind the rest, Helmut crying loudly from the confusion. Maria took the young boy in her arms.

Kurt was intrigued by the sudden mysterious blast. "What was the explosion from, Papa?"

Georg thought for a moment. "It could be that one of our planes crashed. If it were an enemy plane, the sirens would be on."

"But we didn't hear any plane before the explosion," Kurt responded.

"Maybe a wine vat blew up!" said Ruth with a giggle. No one else seemed to think it was humorous.

There had been no other explosion for several minutes, and Georg was becoming more curious. "Kurt, let's go up and try to find out what happened," he said. Kurt joined him eagerly. "We'll be back in a couple of minutes, Maria."

Outside on the street they found Herr Z___ and several other men discussing the event. Georg asked as he approached them, "Does anybody know what that explosion was?"

Z___ seemed distraught. "I think it was a bomb planted by an enemy of the Reich—probably a Jew. I hope he is publicly hanged!"

Herr K___, another neighbor, commented, "Maybe it is a new weapon that the Allies invented. But if so, how are we going to be safe from a bomb that no one knows is coming?" The group stood in tense silence for moment.

"Well, I don't know about you men, but we're going back to the cellar for a while," Georg announced. He turned toward the house and Kurt followed.

Georg entered the cellar and reported, "I don't think—"

"Sh-h-h," Maria whispered. "Helmut is sleeping."

Georg lowered his voice. "I don't think anyone really knows what the explosion was. Let's stay here, just to be safe. Why don't we get some sleep?" The four settled down on the straw mattresses. Suddenly, another boom shook the family to consciousness. This explosion sounded farther away than the first. Still no sirens sounded. Fifteen minutes later, they heard a faint rustling sound, and a third blast splintered the silence—no airplanes, no warning.

"Georg, we must pray!" Maria pleaded. "We don't know how much danger we're in." He nodded, and they all knelt on the dirt floor. The family remained in the cellar the rest of the night.

The following morning, Georg doubled his efforts to find out what had happened. The only facts available were that the explosions came from aerial bombs and that twenty-four people had been killed. Further rumors were abundant.

The people of the city apprehensively went to bed that evening. The Ziefles stayed in the cellar. Their precautions were not in vain. Between 10:30 and 11:00 that night, two more of the mysterious bombs fell on their city.

Many people began commuting to other towns each night rather than endangering themselves in their own homes. The danger was fearsome enough without adding the uncertainty of its origins. As the rumors gained momentum, the people of the Heilbronn gave a name to their phantom attacker—*Bombenkarle,* "Bombing Charlie." He was reputed to be a former Jewish resident of the city who had been expelled by the Nazis and was now gaining revenge by hitting selected targets. *Bombenkarle* did not visit on the third night, which only multiplied the people's suspense.

The quiet night was a relief to the Ziefles, but the following day was Kurt's scheduled departure. His anticipation of the new adventure had weakened during the events of the past few days.

"I wish I could stay home and help," he confessed as the family ate their breakfast. "This *Bombenkarle* business worries me." Maria's sadness at losing another son gained sudden momentum when Kurt voiced his desire to remain home. Her prayers for his soul were having their effect, but soon he would be entering an environment where God was an embarrassment.

Lord, You alone can help him now. It was bad enough when he wanted to go, but now Your seed of love is sprouting in his heart. Don't let it die!

Maria rose to get her Bible from the bookshelf. She sat down, opened the Book, and waited for the rest to be silent. As she read solemnly from Psalm 91—"He that dwelleth in the secret place . . ."—Maria's selection took on special meaning to the sober little family group.

"Now, Kurt, we are going to pray for God to keep you while you are in the Air Force." To Maria's amazement, Kurt accepted the prayer with enthusiasm. The week's mysterious attacker had made a profound change in his attitude.

The family again made the sad expedition to the streetcar stop. Helmut was very fond of his big brother Kurt, and they had often spent time together entertaining each other. Helmut walked beside him that morning, holding his brother's hand tightly. Finally, the little fellow blurted, "Please, Kurt, can't I go with you?"

Kurt chuckled at his small brother. "I don't think they allow little boys in the barracks. But don't worry, I'm sure I'll be able to come home and visit you once in a while."

"But who will I play with when you're not here?"

"You play with the other little boys in the neighborhood. Besides, you're five now, and you must learn to take care of yourself."

Helmut was not convinced, but the streetcar was rumbling toward them, so he had no time to argue. Georg circled Kurt's shoulder with one arm, grabbed his hand, and pumped it warmly as he tried to hold back the tears rising in his own eyes. The rest wept freely as they put their arms around him; Helmut took hold of Kurt's legs from behind.

Maria kissed her son. Then, gazing into his eyes, she whispered, "You will be in my prayers—every day." "Thank you, Mama," he replied, his voice quivering. He raised his voice over the loud squeal of the braking streetcar. "I will miss you! I love you all!" He leaped on board and handed his fare to the conductor. The car lurched forward and clattered slowly down the street as the family waved sorrowfully. The familiar sense of loss was no easier the second time than it had been the first. In spite of the beautiful weather, it was a silent and miserable walk home.

Bombenkarle visited again that evening, dropping two bombs shortly after eight o'clock. Seven people were killed. The Nazis took full advantage of the rumors, which they had no doubt originated, implying Jewish responsibility for the bombings.

The vicious rumors stirred Maria's heart and called forth memories of her Jewish acquaintances, who had been forced unceremoniously out of their homes for "resettlement" in the east. No one seemed to protest. The incessant propaganda had worked.

Maria wondered what had happened to these people. She had heard nothing about them since they left. Someday she would know.

I wish I knew how to pray for them. They are chosen people—Your people, God. But they are treated like criminals. We never hear the whole truth of what the Nazis are doing to them. We suffer for Your sake, but I sense their lot is much, much worse. Be merciful to the Nazis, for they do not even realize their insanity; but, dear God, deliver Your chosen people!

Bombenkarle never struck there again, and the citizens of Heilbronn remained uninformed as to the origin of the attacks. The Nazi leaders were unwilling to reveal that the Allies had developed a superior weapon—a pilotless plane controlled by ultrashortwaves. Flying at an altitude of almost thirty thousand feet, the airplanes entered German territory undetected, then released their deadly payload eight miles from the target. Fortunately for the people of Heilbronn, the devices had been relatively inaccurate in hitting the railroad center, but the psychological effect of the silent destroyer was quite devastating.

Many people, however, remained oblivious to the mounting danger to Germany itself and were still convinced that the Third Reich was invincible. One morning, Maria was conversing with her neighbor, Frau K___, in front of the Ziefle home. Convinced that Germany was heading for inevitable defeat, Maria carefully expressed her doubts, but Frau K___ obstinately denied the possibility.

"Frau Ziefle, how can you be so pessimistic?" Her voice hinted of arrogance. "The Führer promises that we will win this war. It won't be long before he will unveil his new miracle weapon; then the enemy will be defeated!"

"Only God can give us miracles. He is the only One who can protect us. We must put our trust in Him."

Frau K___ lifted her chin proudly. "Not me! Hitler is the only one I can trust! Who needs God?" She stared sharply at Maria, pointing her finger as she continued. "If I were you, I'd get rid of such a critical attitude. We don't like people who are not with us one hundred percent. You've put yourself in a dangerous position."

"You think I'm a traitor to my country." Maria's voice was adamant. "I love Germany. I don't want our country to be defeated. I just know that all the troubles we've faced in the last year are signs that we are not as powerful as we thought we were."

"Humph! Our willpower is strong—we will overcome any obstacles. As long as we are united in love and service to the Führer, nothing can stop us!"

Maria turned toward the front door in an attempt to finish this

City Hall in Sontheim, where Nazis wanted to beat up Georg Ziefle because of his anti-Nazi stand.

uncomfortable conversation. "Please excuse me, but I must feed Helmut now. It is already past his lunchtime." She mounted a step and turned the doorknob.

"Wait and see!" the other woman's shrill voice rang out. "Soon all our enemies will be defeated. Heil Hitler!"

Maria entered and trudged up the stairs. "Miracle weapons!" she muttered. "The Nazis can't even provide us with enough food—and they keep taking our antiaircraft guns to the front!" She laughed as she wagged her head. "What are *we* supposed to use for miracle weapons to protect Sontheim—cabbages?"

She felt the pressure from the Nazis everywhere. This unpleasant confrontation reminded her of an event that had taken place during the summer. Herr Taubenberger, the Nazi branch leader in Sontheim had summoned her husband to appear in City Hall. The Nazis had always hated Georg, and they demanded that he should come to the Party office. He did not know what they had in mind. Yet, when they locked the doors behind him and wanted to beat him up, he said in a fearless and commanding voice that they should open the doors right away or he would inform his superior, Dr. Graner, who was expecting him for work. They opened the doors right away. This time they left him alone because they respected Dr. Graner and Georg's faithful performance at the Red Cross Station I in Heilbronn. For his service he had also received the *Kriegsverdienstkreuz 2. Klasse,* or Second Class Distinguished War Service Cross, on October 21, 1944, as a patrolman of the air-raid protection police. But what good was all of that if they would attack him next time? Because of his criticism of the Nazis, would they not only beat him but also lock him up and kill him perhaps?

Lord, we are so helpless. We need Your protection more than ever.

While she thought about this personal confrontation between her husband and the Nazis and the bad consequences that could result from it, her thoughts returned to her conversation with Frau K___ and the increasingly dangerous military situation. She knew that defense was now a pathetic joke. Only twelve light antiaircraft guns remained to protect the entire Heilbronn area. Gradually, more of the citizens began to sense how vulnerable they really were. Since the *Bombenkarle* scare, the Heilbronn area had not been attacked, but southern German cities were being hit with greater and greater frequency by low-flying Allied fighter-bombers. As winter drew closer, the wailing of the sirens became a daily ordeal; in November, the alarms were sounded ninety-nine times—the Ziefles were running for shelter day and night. Many people, weary of the continued precautions, ignored the warnings carelessly.

The nightly interruptions to her sleep were fatiguing Maria. They had also taken their toll on Ruth, and once she announced angrily, "I don't care if our house is hit. I remain in bed!" Helmut was affected even more. The incessant eerie wails of the sirens had made him so nervous that he would run crying to his mother's bed whenever they awakened him.

Because of the increasing threat, the Ziefles were now taking refuge in public shelters, which seemed to be safer than their cellar. This made readiness more necessary, so Maria began putting Helmut to bed fully clothed. Often, they made use of the underground shelter near the Matthäuskirche; at other times, they resorted to open-air sanctuary among the trees along the Deinenbach, a brook on the east side of Sontheim.

When the alarm sounded again on the night of November 24, Maria decided to take Ruth and Helmut to safety along the Deinenbach. The air was cold, but the silvery moonlight offered a beautiful evening to wait outdoors rather than in a stuffy, overcrowded vault. But it was an air raid, nevertheless, and she wished that Georg were there to accompany them.

Many other people stood nervously in the darkness. Gloomy shadows from trees and humans aggravated Helmut's uneasiness, and he clung to his mother's legs, shivering and whimpering.

A deep droning sounded in the distance, coming closer and growing louder. Although it was more than twenty miles away, the roar of hundreds of enemy bombers was easily recognizable. Just south of Heilbronn, signal rockets, intended to confuse the enemy and prevent the city from being struck, exploded brightly in the sky and descended slowly like balloons as they illuminated the countryside below. Helmut, thrilled with the spectacle, began jumping up and down and shouting at each new burst of light.

The southern horizon began to glow with orange light, punctuated by frequent bright bursts; Stuttgart was under attack.

"May God have mercy on them," said a man standing nearby. But the relative nearness of the burning city reminded them all of their own defenseless predicament. The muffled booming continued as the people watched in awe. Their hearts all wrestled with the same question—when and where would the planes strike next?

War decides between the existence or the nonexistence of the German people. It requires a determined effort by each individual. . . .

—Adolf Hitler

seven

December 4, 1944

SUPPER WAS ALMOST READY AS Georg trudged up the stairs and into the living room that early December evening. Maria stepped out of the kitchen to greet him. Without removing his coat, he sprawled on the couch and sighed, "I hope we don't have another alarm tonight. That one at 4:30 made five so far today. I was trying to transport those wounded soldiers who arrived on the hospital train, and all the alarms made the job twice as hard. But we finally got them all moved—102 of them. I'm exhausted."

Maria smiled and answered, "I hope you can get some rest too. And I made your favorite—the pork chops you bought from that farmer the other day." She returned to the kitchen.

"Where are Ruth and Helmut, Maria?"

"They should be back any moment. They went for a walk. Ruth told me that she had wanted to attend the movies with her friends tonight after school, but the teacher kept them so late the movie had already started. Her friends went anyway, but she decided to come on home. I'm glad, because she didn't have permission to go."

Just then, the two children entered the house. "Hello, Papa!" they exclaimed.

"Come and eat," Maria's voice called from the kitchen. Heilbronn and its suburbs were at that moment bustling with people returning from work, shopping, attending the movie theaters, and waiting for trains to take them on trips. The constant air-raid warnings had become a mere inconvenience; living daily with danger and death had callused their concern.

But as the Ziefles gathered around the supper table and the citizens pursued work and pleasure, a young Russian woman, a captive laborer who lived in Heilbronn but worked in Sontheim, returned from work to the home of her house parents in Heilbronn between 6 and 7 P.M. Her steps were hurried as she entered the house and descended quietly to the cellar. Puzzled because she didn't want to leave the cellar, even for supper, her hostess went down and confronted her.

"What's wrong? What are you doing down here?"

Nervously, the girl replied, "Heilbronn will be destroyed tonight. I am staying down here." No one ever discovered how some foreign workers received advanced warning.

Georg was in the middle of his prayer for the family's supper. The low-pitched growl of sirens coming alive stopped him. He jumped up and went for his coat, filled with fresh vigor in the face of the duties ahead of him. "I'll eat supper when I come back. I've got to go."

Maria called, "Why don't you take two pork chops along and eat them on the way?" She hurried out to him, wrapping the meat in brown paper.

"Thank you, Maria!" He kissed her quickly, then kissed Ruth and Helmut, who were donning their wraps. "I'll see you later!" He ran outside and mounted his bicycle. It was 6:55 P.M., December 4.

Maria and the children bustled out the door and into the street. As they hurried down Ackermannstrasse toward the shelter, the full alarm sounded. As the air began vibrating with the thunder of warplanes, the three (Maria, Ruth, and Helmut) quickened their pace to reach the larger shelter at the Matthäuskirche. Rumbling aircraft engines shook the ground beneath their hurried footsteps. When they reached the end of Ackermannstrasse and turned left to Hauptstrasse, Maria stopped, frozen with fright. Twin-engine Mosquitoes were directly over them. These were fast-flying fighter-bombers that dropped their *Christbäumchen,* or "Christmas trees," the nickname used for these magnesium bombs, to illuminate the target area for the following bombardment. Their floodlights were shining on the streets and rooftops.

Lord, if they drop their bombs now, we're all dead!

When Helmut, who had been fascinated by the beauty of these *Christbäumchen* in the sky at first, learned that they were in great danger, he

Main street in Sontheim (Grocery Lichdi, left) where a policeman cranked his portable siren as Maria, Ruth, and Helmut were racing to the main air-raid shelter on December 4, 1944.

became very frightened and cried out, "Jesus! Help us! Please!" Ruth whimpered fearfully.

Maria grabbed the two children's hands and began running. It seemed so futile. They were hopelessly illuminated by the lights as they ran down the street.

God, we need You as never before!

The streets were nearly empty; most people had already found safety. A policeman stood on the sidewalk near the Lichdi grocery store furiously cranking his portable siren. It was then when God answered Helmut's prayer. As he realized that neither his mother, his sister, nor any other human being could save him if the bombers would drop their bombs now, God quieted his heart and assured him with an inner voice that he would be all right and that he would not have to die. He has never forgotten the closeness of God during those perilous minutes and to feel His presence and protective hands then has been a great encouragement to him throughout his life.

House of cooper master Ludwig Hehn (left) where Maria, Ruth, and Helmut stayed in his
air-raid shelter during the Heilbronn air raid on December 4, 1944.

The three Ziefles had no time to reach the shelter near the church, so they
headed to another one that was closer, the deep cellar of cooper master Hehn.
At this time—as Ruth remembers—suddenly a strong wind sprang up and
drove away the *Christbäumchen* in the direction of Heilbronn. If the wind had
not come up, they would have been hit on this street by the release of incendiary
and high-explosive bombs. For some unknown reason, however, the planes
had not yet dropped any bombs. When the night was over, it would be
obvious—their target was Heilbronn, not Sontheim. Two hundred and fifty-
five Lancaster bombers were flying in columns on either side of Heilbronn. A
few miles east of the city, they would make the turn that would bring them
back to unleash their hellish cargo.

The cooperage of Küferei Hehn trembled from the awesome bellowing of
the returning Lancasters. Its eighty occupants sat or stood in fearful silence,

Group picture of Lancaster bomber crews who attacked Heilbronn on December 4, 1944, with Lancaster bomber in background. A total of 255 Lancaster bombers dropped 1,150 tons of bombs and incendiary and highly explosive ammunition on Heilbronn.

various emotional responses etched on their faces. Death was near at hand. The air-raid warden standing near the large steel door glanced at his watch in the dim light of battery lanterns—it was 7:15.

The low-flying Mosquito fighters continued to swoop over the buildings. The war-weary people, although enclosed in the shelter, could imagine the crackling magnesium illumination bombs that bath the blacked-out city with a bright, greenish glow. A few minutes later, the deafening roar of the Lancasters was split by the explosions of 1,150 tons of incendiary bombs and heavy explosives hitting their targets.

In spite of her previous experiences, Maria could hardly believe the ear-splitting roar and the shock of the explosions. People screamed and pointed at the heavy steel door at the entrance, which, with each wave of explosions, bulged like paper in the wind. All around Maria, people were on their knees crying out to God. One man, hands over his ears, shouted continuously, "God, forgive! Save me! Lord, have mercy on me!"

A woman next to him mumbled softly as she frantically fingered the beads of her rosary.

Others clawed hysterically at the concrete walls, as if attempting to climb out. Maria stared with helpless compassion at these people who before had arrogantly denied the Creator's power.

Helmut, wide-eyed, observed the terror of the people around him. The continual races to the shelter and his innocent faith had finally stiffened his tolerance for these frightening events.

The rumbling of the planes began to recede. It was 7:45 P.M. The still sporadic explosions continued all night because many of the bombs were timed to detonate after impact, some as much as ten hours later. But the people in the air-raid shelter were beginning to calm.

Maria was anxious to go home to see if her house was safe. She also wanted fresh air. But it was the warden's responsibility to decide when they could leave. She remembered a pamphlet that the government had issued earlier in the year informing the citizens that they should wait in the air-raid bunkers for up to five hours to ensure their safety. She put the warning out of her mind and heard with relief the warden's instructions that allowed them to go.

The group filed outside—and gaped in horror, shielding their eyes. The inner city of Heilbronn was a blinding fireball. Maria pleaded quietly, *Lord, put Your angels around Georg tonight. Don't let that inferno swallow him up. Be merciful to us all.*

Holding tightly to Ruth and Helmut's hands, Maria carefully picked her way homeward. As they turned east at Heilbronner Strasse, they collided with a staggering mass of smoke-blackened people fleeing from Heilbronn into Sontheim. It looked like a death march. A woman ran frantically toward the Ziefles and grabbed Maria's arm. Her coat was partially burned, and she was covered with dirt and soot. "Frau, please help me!" she begged. "Our house was hit, and the rest of my family was killed! Please!" Maria did not even ask the woman's name. Letting go of Ruth, she placed her arm behind the woman and led her toward home—if it indeed was still there.

The four of them turned off Ackermannstrasse and hastened anxiously past the Scholterer's home. Their house was there and intact! With thanks in her heart, Maria led her group into the house. The woman in Maria's arms kept whimpering, "I want to die too. Why wasn't I killed?"

The four filed upstairs to the kitchen. The unfinished supper was still on the table. And the coffee was still warm. Although there was no electricity, the orange glow from the city provided sufficient light in the room so that they could see each other. Exhausted, they forced themselves to eat. The stranger could not get over having lost her entire family and her home in less than an hour and a half; she was now totally on her own. Her husband, two children, and a cousin had been killed when a bomb exploded beside their house. Still in shock, the woman looked blankly around her. Maria led her to the living room, helped her lie down on the couch, and put a blanket over her. She fell immediately into a deep stupor.

Maria sat down again at the kitchen table. "Helmut, Ruth, let's pray for your papa now. I'm sure he's in great danger." The three bowed their heads and took turns imploring God to protect their beloved father. Maria added a plea for their guest in the living room. When Maria finished, they all prepared for bed.

Lying beneath the eiderdown comforter, Ruth thought restlessly of all of her classmates who were no doubt in the movie theater when the planes arrived.

Did they get out? Did they find shelter? I would have been there without my parents' permission. Would God have protected me? She would not know until morning.

❧

Fifty miles south of Heilbronn in Dettingen, Teck, two Air Force trainees were strolling toward the barracks. "Look," one of them said, "is that a fire in the north?"

"Must have been a bombing, Rolf."

"I suppose it must be about twenty miles away. Ludwigsburg, maybe, eh, Kurt?"

"You're probably right. I feel sorry for those people." The two stared at the orange glow for a few seconds, then proceeded into the barracks.

❧

The brilliance of the nearby inferno illuminated her bedroom as Maria attempted to sleep. She wondered about friends and relatives who lived in the vicinity. And she prayed again, especially for Georg. Georg had reached the Red Cross station while the planes were still making their first pass over the city. He hurried into the workers' room of the air-raid shelter and sat anxiously waiting for the other ambulance drivers to arrive. He shivered from the vibrations of the airplane engines as he pulled the pork chops from his coat pocket.

A man dashed through the door. It was his partner, Karl Wieland. "Karl!" Georg exclaimed. "Where are the other drivers?"

Karl stared at him, his eyes big with fear. "No one else has arrived? Some of the men live closer to the station than we do."

Incendiary bombs rain down on Heilbronn near Hotel "Central" on December 4, 1944.

"Dr. Hofherr, and a couple of nurses are here—but that's all. Maybe some of them were too scared to come out."

The drone of the planes was suddenly broken by the staccato of dozens of incendiary bombs clattering like hail on a sheet-metal roof. Deafening blasts shook the bunker; several bombs had fallen very close by. The building shuddered violently. The lights flickered and went out.

Karl cried out in the blackness, "Georg, I'm afraid to die! Pray for me!"

"Don't worry, Karl, I already have!" Georg shouted above the roar of the planes and explosions. "God is going to protect us! Be brave—we have a big job to do tonight!"

Five waves of Lancasters unleashed their deadly fury upon the city. Georg and Karl sat helplessly in the room, wondering if their wives and children were still alive. The sound of planes thinned into the distance, although the timed explosions continued the destruction. Dr. Hofherr, holding a flashlight, came running into the shelter.

"Georg, Karl, we must get our lights back on. I can't give treatment using only flashlights and candles." He sounded desperate. "Do you know how to start the auxiliary generator? Willi isn't here to do it."

Georg jumped to his feet. "I've never done it before, but I've watched Willi start it several times. I'll run outside and see what I can do."

Georg hurried upstairs and stepped out into the blazing night. All around him were shattered houses being gutted by flames. He took a few steps toward the vehicle garage where the generator was housed. He stopped in dismay. Flames were pouring from the roof of the building.

Georg whirled and ran back down to the shelter. Karl was just coming up the stairway. "Karl, the garage is on fire! You'll have to help me if we're going to start the generator."

"How bad is the fire?" Karl countered. Georg ran up the steps and Karl followed him outside. He stared at the blaze. "I'm not going in there with you! I don't want to be a dead hero."

"Karl!" Georg was angry. "People's lives will depend on the light that generator provides! Some of those people might even be your own family!"

Karl shrugged his shoulders weakly and nodded. Georg sprinted toward the garage and Karl ran close behind him. They dashed through the door and peered through the smoke. Every vehicle was destroyed—except theirs.

"Get our ambulance out away from the flames," Georg barked. "I'll start on the generator. Come back and help me when you're done."

The men separated. Georg turned up the collar on his jacket and hurtled through a maze of fallen beams and bricks. The generator stood silently in the glow of the flames; it was far enough from the flames to be safe! He took a deep breath, bent low and ran toward it, the heat tearing at his lungs.

He reached for the controls and pulled the choke. He fumbled for the crank, inserted it, and gave it three violent jerks. Nothing. He ran frantically outside for cool air. Karl was stepping out of the ambulance.

"Karl, come and help me!"

"I'm not going back in that furnace!" he argued.

"Well, then, stand at the door and keep an eye on me. If I need help, you'll be ready." Karl consented.

Georg dove back into the smoke and rubble, trying to avoid breathing the poisonous air. He reached the generator and grabbed the crank. He whirled it viciously. The engine sputtered; he desperately adjusted the choke. It revived. He closed the switch to the power line and the generator howled into action.

As Georg ran back to the building, the first bombing victims staggered toward the center. They were a frightening lot. Some of them were covered with wet clothes as protection from the heat. Many of them shielded their faces with handkerchiefs, hoping to save their lungs from the acrid fumes. Soon, more than a hundred people had crowded into the waiting room. Georg and Karl tried to help the injured settle themselves. They laid on pallets those who had the worst burns.

Dr. Hofherr stepped into the room to survey the work ahead of him. Spotting Georg, he called, "Ziefle, thanks for starting the generator. That will save many lives tonight." Georg nodded and smiled as the doctor continued, "I think you should start out with the ambulance. Is yours ready?" Georg realized suddenly the miracle that had occurred with his vehicle.

"All were destroyed, except mine, Doctor. We'll leave right away." He and Karl hurried out the door and toward their van.

Georg turned the ambulance into the street. Directly in front of them lay a woman. The two jumped out and ran to her side. Her mouth and nose were full of ashes, and she was gasping for breath. The men quickly cleaned the debris from her air passages and she regained her breath. They helped her into the back of their van and drove to the door of the center. They had made their first rescue, and they had hardly left the Red Cross station.

The men drove slowly through the streets not only to avoid running over the thousands of people who were fleeing the city but also to spot as many victims as possible whom they could help. They stopped and administered first aid wherever it was needed. The streets were now just rubble-strewn alleys between walls of fire. As they turned a corner, the street before them was filled with flames from a collapsed building. Concerned for the people who

A fleeing person runs for his life through the firestorm during the air attack on Heilbronn, December 4, 1944. He runs past Hotel "Vaterland" covered by a blanket (very likely wet) for extra protection from sparks.

might be trapped on the other side, Georg downshifted and accelerated the vehicle, careening wildly through the flaming rubble.

"Georg! Are you crazy! You'll kill both of us!" Karl cried.

"This isn't a Sunday drive, Karl! People's lives are at stake!" In seconds, they had cleared the scorching maze. "Thank you, Lord!" he whispered.

Before long, the ambulance was full, and Georg drove the van as quickly as he could to the Red Cross station. He and Karl unloaded the victims and began their third trip.

This time, the men were almost downtown. Hundreds of fires had combined and engulfed the entire area. The glaring heat sent hurricane-like blasts of scorching air among the burning buildings. That anyone could still be alive in there seemed impossible. Grief welled up in Georg's heart as he thought of the people who were trapped in those once-beautiful buildings and who would be only ashes by morning.

Suddenly, a figure stumbled out of the flames toward the ambulance. It was a man with a blanket over his body. The blanket was burning. Georg opened his door as the man fell almost in front of the van. Georg and Karl rushed to him and tore the blanket from him. They carefully helped the man into the ambulance. He was badly burned, but he would live.

As they ground to a halt after spotting another victim, a large "thump" sounded from the vehicle's undercarriage. The two paid no attention—the streets were full of debris. As Georg and Karl bent over the victim, a policeman ran up behind them yelling, "Are you guys trying to get killed? You just drove over a bomb!" The two men froze and stared at each other. Georg finally managed a wry smile. "I think we have angels around our ambulance tonight!" Karl nodded weakly.

The van full again, they returned to the station, and in a matter of minutes they had unloaded the van and were on their way. They threaded their way along a wide boulevard divided by large trees. But tonight it was a grisly spectacle. People, their clothing ablaze, ran down the street, screaming in agony. In desperation, many of them embraced the trees, as if pleading for help, but they died as human torches. Georg watched anxiously for those who could be saved.

The city of Heilbronn flamed and roared like a gigantic blowtorch. Beneath the city, thousands of people cowered, dutifully obeying the government's instructions to remain in the bunkers as long as possible. Several of the shelters were torn open by the suction of the heat and delayed bomb explosions. Flames and poisonous gases swept over the hapless victims and devoured them.

In other shelters, carbon monoxide seeped in, and the occupants drowsily suffocated. Some survivors in the bunkers became uneasy, sensing their plight, and attempted to climb out through the narrow escape tunnels. Frequently, many such passages were jammed with debris or supplies, and in some instances the escapees were trapped by the bulk of their own luggage. Those following them were caught in the crush and suffocated.

No place was totally safe. Much of the air-raid shelter at Heilbronn's main hospital as well as its occupants was destroyed. Many wounded soldiers whom Georg had transferred that morning were killed when their auxiliary hospital was hit. All of the hospitals in the city were demolished. Only two First-Aid Stations remained—the one on Wilhelmstrasse and another at the Kaiser-Friedrich-Plaza. That night alone, almost eight hundred people received treatment at the Wilhelmstrasse center for wounds, burns, smoke inhalation, and carbon monoxide poisoning. By the next day, others had developed heavy infections in the membranes of their eyes, noses, and throats and also required treatment.

As the sun rose on the following day, Georg continued wearily the back-breaking but rewarding task. Most of the still-walking victims had left the center, but now those requiring hospitalization needed to be transported. In addition to those from the Red Cross station, hundreds of other patients from the Heilbronn hospitals who had survived the bombing needed to be relocated. Many of them were transferred to the Weissenhof facility near Weinsberg—now serving mainly as a hospital—by ambulance, horse-drawn wagon, and pushcart. Dozens arrived dead.

❧

Maria arose that morning feeling more tired than when she had gone to bed. Georg was still not home. The possibility of his being dead clawed at her heart. She could only wait and pray.

Heilbronn had ceased to function as a city. Services, utilities, and businesses were destroyed or crippled. The night of December 4–5, 1944, had been the worst in its history. The survivors began the anxious search for the remains of loved ones. Many people had been burned beyond recognition or were lost in the rubble. The flames had devoured civil and medical records. Not until years later was the count final: almost seven thousand were dead. More than one thousand were children under ten years of age.

We are completely defenseless. The Reich is gradually being transformed into a complete desert. Göring is responsible with his Luftwaffe. It is no longer capable of conducting defensive operations.

—Joseph Goebbels

eight

December 5, 1944

THE TWO AIR FORCE TRAINEES AT Dettingen, Teck, sat nonchalantly eating their breakfast in the mess hall.

"Say, Ziefle!" a voice called from an adjoining table. "I heard Heilbronn was bombed last night. Isn't that where you're from?"

Kurt, ashen-faced, turned to Rolf. Rolf was from Böckingen, another Heilbronn suburb. Their forks fell from their limp hands. "We've got to go home and check on our families! Let's go see the commander, Rolf." The two scrambled away from the table and out of the room. They had felt pity last night when they thought that the flames were rising from Ludwigsburg; now they were filled with near panic.

Much to their relief, the commander willingly granted the pair overnight passes. He had heard that the fiery glow from Heilbronn was witnessed from as far away as Ulm—nearly one hundred miles away. He could only advise the two anxious young men to expect the worst. Tense with the fear of never seeing their families again, Kurt and Rolf ran to the station to catch the earliest train home.

❧

Rubbing her eyes and fighting the weariness in her body, Maria dragged herself upstairs to fix breakfast for her family. Passing through the living room, she stepped toward the couch to check on the stranger. The blanket was heaped at one end, and no one was in the room. Maria glanced around. The woman's coat and shoes were not there. The events of the night had nearly suffocated Maria's spirit, yet concern for the destitute woman welled up in her heart.

God, be merciful to that poor woman. I don't know if she is wandering in the streets or is with friends, but she has lost everything. Somehow, let her sense Your love. We may have entertained an angel in our midst.

Breakfast for the three Ziefles was a simple meal eaten slowly and silently. With Heilbronn in shambles and Georg's safety in question, there seemed no purpose in hurrying to face the day. Ruth, like her mother, had slept poorly, having spent the night wondering if her schoolmates had escaped the bombing. Helmut was the only one who had energy.

Finally, Maria broke the silence. "We really need to find out if your father is all right. I'm wondering if I should take Helmut with me and walk to the Red Cross station this morning." She stared pensively at the window. "But what would happen if the planes attacked again? We might not reach a shelter in time."

Ruth leaned forward in her chair. "Mama, why don't you let me go and find out about Papa? If I rode my bike, I could get there in half the time."

"It's very dangerous for a girl to be alone out there."

"Don't worry, Mama. I'll be careful. Please."

Maria hesitated and then nodded with a slight smile. Ruth jumped from her chair, grabbed her coat, and headed for the door.

Reaching the Red Cross center took much longer than usual. Two or three streets farther from the Kamerawerk, which was about half way between Sontheim and Heilbronn, she already noticed the first bomb craters. The closer she got, the greater was the destruction. Starting from the Südbahnhof, a train station that was close to her father's Red Cross station, there were more and more heaps of ruins. Across from Red Cross Station I, the soap factory Flammer lay in ruins. The more she grasped the extent of the destruction, the more it dashed her hope of seeing her father alive again. She needed an answer now. She leaned her bike against the wall and ran to the door of the Red Cross station. When she entered, a nurse rushed past her. Ruth grabbed the nurse's arm desperately and gasped, "Tell me! Is my father still alive?"

The nurse, obviously exhausted from the long night, replied briefly, "Who are you?"

"Ruth Ziefle."

"Oh! You are Herr Ziefle's daughter!" The woman's countenance was suddenly exuberant. "He's still picking up injured people all over the city. Your father is a hero, did you know that? If it were not for him, our center wouldn't even be operating. He risked his life to start up the generator."

Her anxiety now turned to joy, Ruth asked eagerly, "Will he be able to come home soon?"

"That I can't promise. All of us here are exhausted, and we hope to go home later today. It depends on how soon some others can come to replace us."

"Tell him we're happy that he's all right—and that we love him!" Ruth rushed out the door joyfully.

Before she returned home, she wanted to go by all means in the direction of downtown to her school and pick up the school utensils she had there. Because it was so difficult to make headway, she left her bike at the Red Cross station and went on foot. Everywhere she looked, she saw only piles of debris, bomb craters, duds, and heaps of stones. She had either to go around them or to climb over them. It was simply terrible. But then she noticed something that left an indelible impression on her. Along Hohestrasse she saw hundreds of small corpses lined up closely at the road. The dead were completely charred and shrunk so much that they looked like mummies in the form of large dolls. The residents had fled to the street and were scorched there. Ruth simply could not comprehend that so many people had to die here so cruelly. A policeman said to her, "Fräulein, this is no place for you to be!"

In a daze, she continued to stumble in the direction of the *Chemieschule*, the school where she studied chemistry. Also, here and there in the park of the *Friedenskirche*, or Church of Peace, lay charred corpses and pieces of scorched cloth. From there, she also saw the part of the school where her classroom was. Yet, the path was blocked by ruins, and she could not pick up her school utensils. Ruth was completely exhausted by the sight of all of this misery, and she set out for home. She returned first to the Red Cross station to meet her father, but he was still on duty. She took her bike and hurried to take her mother the good news of her father's survival and his courageous effort.

Wending her way home, Ruth could take more time for reflection. She was amazed at how quickly the people of Heilbronn were rallying after the disaster.

Rows of corpses in Lammgasse (alley) in Heilbronn after air attack on Heilbronn on December 4, 1944.

They were busy moving rubble, searching for bodies, and attempting to return some sense of normalcy to the city. The job ahead of them was monstrous. Almost all public facilities had been demolished, including the fire stations. Water and gas lines were broken in hundreds of places. Work crews streamed in to help with cleanup and restoration. Some crews came from as far away as the Ruhr Valley, three hundred miles to the northwest.

But the fate of her classmates who had gone to see a movie in the Ufa-Movie Theater on December 4 was still very much on her mind. Did any of them survive? She didn't know until about a day later when a girlfriend told her that all of her classmates who had gone to see the movie had perished. A troop of miners from the Ruhr District equipped with special carbon monoxide detection equipment had found them after a long and exhausting effort in the cellar below the movie theater. Without exception, they were dead. Ruth was almost numb for a moment. She knew now that she would have been dead too, if she hadn't obeyed her mother, who had told her not go to the movies. She knew that it was the Lord's hand that had protected her and saved her life.

After the initial shock, Ruth regained her composure and said to her girl-friend, "It's hard for me to believe this, but it must be true after I have seen the terrible destruction in Heilbronn. It must have been a terrible death for my classmates, and it's hard for me to imagine that I will never see them again. It is so tragic." The girlfriend tried to console Ruth as much as she could, but she could not forget the fate of her classmates for the rest of her life.

❧

But peace had not yet returned, and no one knew what the next day would bring. Allied planes were attacking German targets relentlessly, trying to force the Reich to its knees. Although Heilbronn, for the time being, was quiet, other areas were not. Kurt and Rolf's train, past Ludwigsburg, was pursued by fighter-bombers. Fortunately, the train was entering a tunnel, and the quick-thinking engineer brought the train to a halt once it was inside the mountain. The bombers, however, blasted the other end of the tunnel, sealing it shut. Unwilling to turn back, Kurt and Rolf walked ten miles to Bietigheim. Because the track to Heilbronn was damaged, they took a train to Marbach instead, from where they could get to Sontheim on a smaller narrow-gage train. There they encountered several people on their way back to the Heilbronn area. To Kurt and Rolf's relief, the people assured them that only Heilbronn proper, not the suburbs, was hit during the raid. Their spirits lifted, the two waited impatiently for the train to arrive.

❧

It was nearly time for supper when Georg finally came home to rest for the night. As he ate his meal, he spoke little of his tireless efforts to save many lives. He was more concerned about the plight of the wounded, homeless, widowed, and orphaned. As Maria observed her husband, she tried to remember the dark-haired, vigorous man he had been before the war. The gray hair and the lines in his face were only outward indications of the toll that the war had taken. She was certain that he would never be the same man after the ordeal of the last twenty-four hours. He had seen death as few men ever had.

As the four finished their thin gruel, Maria announced, "Because Papa needs to get his rest, we will have *Dämmerstündle* now rather than later."

She looked at her youngest. "Helmut, which Bible story would you like to hear tonight?"

Helmut brightened with importance and readied his answer. But the closing of the front door and the sound of footsteps stole the family's attention. They looked at each other, puzzled.

Georg rose from his chair and stepped toward the stairway. "Who's there?" he called apprehensively.

"It's me!" a voice rang back.

"Kurt!" the family chorused. The three at the table sprang to their feet and joined Georg and Kurt in happy embraces.

With their arms around her son, Maria cried out inwardly, *Why are we allowed such joy when others are left with nothing? Why, Lord, have we been spared?*

The next day, Kurt met Youth Pastor Reininghaus, who asked him to participate in the memorial service for fifteen Sunday school teachers who had lost their lives on December 4. The *Friedenskirche* looked desolate. The tower was completely shelled to pieces and the church was gutted. With difficulty, Kurt and the pastor climbed the stairway to the clock tower. They discovered that one lone bell was still hanging there; however, its rope had burned down to a few yards. Pastor Reininghaus asked Kurt if he would have the courage to ring the bell for the memorial service. He said yes, and it worked. Kurt was the last person who rang this bell. The *Friedenskirche* had to be dynamited later because of the danger of its collapsing.

Bombed out Friedenskirche (Church of Peace) where, shortly before its demolition, Kurt rang the church bell for a memorial service of Sunday school teachers who had been killed on December 4, 1944.

We shall never capitulate.

—Adolf Hitler

nine

January 1945

IN THE MIDDLE OF JANUARY 1945, the gliding flight school near Teck had been dissolved. Kurt was able to come home for a few days. But he already had the order in his pocket to report at the air base Brünn in Czechoslovakia.

It was almost noon of Kurt's first day home when the air-raid sirens began to howl. Maria was at the stove making pancakes for lunch. The family members scrambled for their coats—all except Kurt, who wanted to enjoy every moment he had of his short stay at home.

Scoffing at the danger, Kurt insisted, "Let's not waste these pancakes, Mama. If we take them off the heat now, they'll never taste as good. You go on to the shelter and I'll finish them."

"Kurt, it's not safe!" his father scolded.

"I can take care of myself, Papa. I'll go to the cellar if it gets too bad."

His parents shrugged their shoulders helplessly. Ruth grabbed the suitcase with their important belongings and hurried for the door. Helmut jumped on Georg's back, and Maria took her husband's arm—her phlebitis had made walking increasingly difficult.

As the Ziefles rushed breathlessly to the shelter, their neighbor with whom they shared the cellar, Frau Krauter, ran into the Ziefle kitchen. Kurt was turning pancakes calmly.

Heilbronn, a city destroyed after December 4, 1944.

"Kurt, I don't want to stay here and die!" she exclaimed, her face pale with fright. "Please go with me to the Deinenbach where it's safer."

Kurt smiled at the distraught woman. "Frau Krauter, I don't think it will be so bad. Besides, I'd rather stay right here."

Frantic, she pulled on Kurt's sleeve. "Please, go with me!" Out of compassion for the woman, Kurt accompanied her.

Fighter-bombers were approaching Sontheim in broad daylight. "Hurry, Frau Krauter!" Kurt yelled as they ran frantically across an open field about two hundred yards from home. They were almost to the brook, the Deinenbach. The roar of the attackers was nearly above them.

Suddenly, the whistle of released bombs shrieked through the air, and Kurt dove into the grass; his elderly neighbor ran on. The deafening blasts surrounded him. The *Staufenbergschule,* only two hundred meters from them, had been hit. Because of the air pressure of the explosions, bricks, tiles, and other projectiles were flying in all directions. Cautiously, Kurt raised himself up for a moment. He was hurled to the ground by a hard blow on his right arm. A piece of a brick had demolished his upper arm.

He needed cover, so he jumped to his feet and ran for the brook. He would have to jump across the water to reach the protection of the trees and bushes. Holding his arm with his left hand, he approached the water at full speed and leaped. His feet slipped on the wet ground, and he landed in the middle of the brook, his full weight on his injured arm. The suffocating pain obliterated any sensation of January cold from the water.

Kurt looked again at his arm. The mangled, bleeding limb hung loosely, connected to his shoulder only by flesh and his hand twisted by 180 degrees. His face turned white. "Lord! Have mercy on me!" he cried aloud. The pain increased, but a new sense of peace came over him as he realized that God was hearing his call for help.

His arm and shoulder throbbing with pain, Kurt struggled to his feet and stumbled through the brook to one of the hollowed-out shelters along the bank. Herr Ritter, an acquaintance of Kurt, approached him, having noticed the youth grimacing with pain. "What happened to you, Kurt?" he asked, shocked as he saw the mangled arm.

"Bomb splinters!" Kurt gasped. "Can you do anything for it until I get to a doctor?"

Staufenbergschule, which was hit during the air raid on Sontheim on January 20, 1945. Flying debris from this school demolished Kurt's upper right arm.

In lieu of medical supplies, the man drew a large handkerchief from his pocket and wrapped it around the open wound. He then made Kurt sit down until the bomb attack subsided.

As soon as the planes began to fly away from the town, Herr Ritter helped Kurt to his feet and walked him to Ackermannstrasse. Every movement was torture; Kurt groaned and clenched his jaws as the burning pain tore through him.

❧

Beneath the ground in their bunker, Georg and Maria waited restlessly for the all clear. Anxiety over Kurt nagged at both of them. Unable to sit any longer, Georg finally turned to his wife. "I have a feeling that something has happened to Kurt. You three stay here and I'll see if I can find him." He rose and hurried out of the shelter.

As Georg reached Ackermannstrasse, his fears were confirmed. Coming from the other direction was Kurt, holding his limp arm, his face white and twisted with pain. Georg ran to his son and immediately examined the arm. He exclaimed, "I've hardly ever seen such a bad fracture. Let's get you to Dr. Schramm."

The two walked as fast as Kurt could manage. Approaching the doctor's house, they halted in dismay. The house and yard were filled with others who had been injured in the attack.

"We can't wait that long," Georg said. "I'll take you to the military hospital. Staff surgeon Braik is on duty, and he'll help you."

"But how will we get to Heilbronn?" Kurt groaned.

"I wish we still had our car," Georg muttered. "And I don't have my ambulance at home. You sit here and wait," he ordered. "I'll go get my bicycle." He ran down the street, and in a few minutes he returned, pedaling furiously.

"You sit on the seat and I'll sit on the bar and pedal," he said to his son.

Kurt swung his leg over the back wheel and tried to perch himself on the saddle. Without any place to rest his feet, balance was impossible. "Papa, this will never work," he insisted. "Let me ride the bike myself."

Georg steadied the bike while Kurt positioned himself. Summoning all of his remaining strength, Kurt held the handlebar with his good arm, pushed on the pedals, and moved away. His father ran behind him for more than a mile.

They made it to Georg's Red Cross station at Wilhelmstrasse, where an additional six wounded were waiting for transport to the hospital. Then they drove in the ambulance to the military hospital near the old cemetery in Heilbronn, where Dr. Braik, a bone specialist, was staff surgeon. Without administering anesthesia, he rotated Kurt's hand to its proper position while his father held the lower arm.

Because Dr. Braik could not treat Kurt's upper arm, Georg drove with Kurt and six other wounded to the hospital at the Weissenhof near Weinsberg. He was admitted on the same day but not treated until a few days later. First, the head physician at the hospital set the upper arm, then he X-rayed it. Three times he tried unsuccessfully to do so; Kurt's bones had been splintered too much by the pieces of brick. After two weeks, the head physician decided to connect the various fractures with a silver nail. Even today Kurt is still 40 percent war disabled.

As Georg and Kurt and the other wounded left Heilbronn in the ambulance, Maria, Ruth, and Helmut arrived back at their home. Stepping inside, they all sniffed, puzzled at the burning smell. Ruth ran upstairs. Soon, her laughter rang from the kitchen.

"What is so funny?" Maria called as she and her son came into the room.

"Look what Kurt left!" Ruth replied, giggling. Seven black pancakes lay on the still-hot stove. Maria shook her head, wondering what had happened to Kurt.

Maria was relieved when she heard from Georg, when he came home, that Kurt had been admitted and treated successfully in the hospital at the Weissenhof. Although it was not a pleasant event, it was still good to realize that Kurt would be delayed in returning to military duty. If only Reinhold could be home as well.

The following day was Sunday, and Maria sent Helmut with Ursula, a neighbor girl, to the nursery school at the *Matthäuskirche*. Maria and Ruth would join him later at the morning service. Georg was on Red Cross duty.

It was almost ten o'clock, and the children's class was getting under way when the sirens began to wail. Frantically, the woman in charge searched for the keys to the interior of the church because the classroom offered little protection.

The planes were overhead already, and the frightened children cowered against a wall. Many of them were crying. Trying her best to calm the group, the sister had them bow their heads, then offered a short prayer. She looked up and asked, "Can any of you also pray for us?" Helmut raised his hand cautiously, then lifted his voice. "Lord, don't let those planes hurt us. And bring us home safely. Amen."

"Thank you, Helmut." She noted the quiet confidence in his large, brown eyes. "Would anyone else like to pray?" None volunteered.

The church was spared from the attack. But in two days' time, more than 160 people were killed in the Heilbronn area.

As Kurt lay in the hospital, not only was his body recovering but also an astounding change had come over his attitude. Georg and Maria were delighted by his spiritual condition when they visited their son to find him reading his Bible, singing hymns, and telling his ten roommates about his experience with God. The Almighty had responded to Kurt's helpless cry as he lay in mortal fear in the cold water of the Deinenbach. God's peace had filled his heart in spite of the pain in his body. This ardent young disciple of the Nazi cause no longer followed the swastika.

Impressed by the encouraging effect that Kurt had on his fellow roommates, one of the nurses suggested that he expand his "ministry" to some of the other patients. Before long, he was reading the Bible, praying, and singing for the patients in seven rooms.

But not even a hospital was free from the anti-God mentality of Nazism. One day as Kurt was singing to some patients, an angry voice growled from behind him, "What's going on in here?"

Kurt turned and looked into the icy eyes of the head physician, Dr. Reichhold, who would later commit suicide with his wife one day after the arrival of the American Army. "I just wanted to encourage my friends with the Word of God and a few hymns," he replied innocently.

"You are disturbing my patients! Get out and don't do this again!"

The patients were as disappointed as Kurt. But he had made a strong impression on them, and they did not forget.

A few days later, another air-raid alarm sounded, and the patients were rushed to the cellar. Some of them were so disquieted that a nurse finally called for Kurt to come and calm them by praying with them.

Eight days had passed since Kurt's injury. It was Tuesday night, February 7, and Maria lay sleepless in her bed, wondering what the week would bring and praying for her family. It was almost midnight.

"Mother!" a voice whispered loudly from outside the window. Someone was knocking on the shutters. "Mother! It's me, Reinhold!"

"Reinhold!" she cried. "I'll be right there!" She shook her husband. "Georg! Reinhold is outside! Go tell the children!" Maria rose from the bed and hurried to unlatch the door.

She pushed the door open and peered at her eldest. His ruddy face was barely visible in the darkness. She flung her arms around him. "Why are you here?" she said softly. "Is something wrong?"

By now, the rest of the family was coming toward the door. Reinhold stepped inside and embraced each one. "I can't stay long. I have to catch up with my unit as fast as I can."

In January 1945, Reinhold's unit had been ordered for action from the Eifel Mountains via the Saarland to the Haguenau Forest, the *Hagenauer Wald,* in Alsace when the Americans were already near Strasbourg. Many of his comrades either froze to death or were killed. They had to be in the open day and night. The food froze in the snow. On Wednesday, February 7, 1945, Reinhold's unit was transferred from Haguenau Forest to the Eastern Front, and during this trip by train he visited his family for the last time before he became a prisoner of war.

"Maria, make him something to eat," Georg said, smiling at his eldest.

"What would you like?" asked Maria.

Reinhold thought a moment. "How about bean stew?"

"I'll fix it right away," his mother assured. "Come up to the kitchen so we can talk."

"How did you get here?" Georg asked as they walked up the stairs.

"As I was on my way from the Western to the Eastern Front at Bietigheim, I found out that our train would not go through Heilbronn as planned. I wanted to come home, so I waited in the bathroom at the station until the train began to pull away. Then I ran out and chased it, even though I knew I wouldn't catch it.

"I approached a station official who had seen me running after the train, and asked for an affidavit. Then I was able to get permission to catch up with my unit via Heilbronn. I got on the next train and jumped off in Böckingen and ran all the way here. I'm lucky no one caught me. I'll have to leave early in the morning to be able to rejoin my unit. If I'm late I could be shot on the spot as a deserter."

"How about hiding here?" Georg suggested. "I'm sure it won't be long before the war is over.

"It's too dangerous, Papa. If I were caught here, we would all be shot."

"You're right," Georg muttered. "There are too many Nazis in the neighborhood."

Maria stood quietly by the stove, stirring the beans. *Lord, why must he be put in such a predicament? If he stays here, he will be killed, and if he goes to the Eastern Front. . . .*

Georg began updating Reinhold about Kurt and his change of heart. Reinhold could hardly contain his joy at the good news. Maria ladled the steaming beans into a bowl and placed it in front of Reinhold. Forcing a smile, she said, "Enjoy it. Eat as much as you can."

Reinhold attacked the food with his spoon. Not waiting until he swallowed, he exclaimed, "This is so good, Mama! You know, I haven't eaten since breakfast?" He continued devouring the stew, then handed the empty bowl to his mother. She smiled and filled it again. Maria glanced at Reinhold's coat, which he had tossed on the chair next to him. Puzzled, she picked it up. "What happened to your coat? It looks like a sieve!"

He put down his spoon and grinned. "Thank the Lord, it was the coat and not me! We left Strasbourg this evening, and between the towns of Bruchsal and Bretten our train was riddled with bullets by machine gunfire from enemy planes. We all ran out and hid in the forest, but I forgot to take my coat. There are a lot of bullet holes in it."

Maria held the shredded coat to her breast. Her eyes glistened and her lips trembled as she whispered, "Lord, You *are* taking care of us!" She paused several seconds to calm herself. "Is there anything else you wish while you're here, Reinhold?"

"Mama, could we have a *Dämmerstündle?* I've been dreaming about it ever since I left home."

"Of course!" Maria replied as she pulled the Bible off the shelf and laid it next to her husband. "But we must be careful not to wake any neighbors. We don't want to arouse any suspicion that you are here."

Georg opened the Scriptures and read a chapter. Then each person prayed.

Emotions peaked as they implored God to protect their son and brother as he went to the Russian Front. A reassuring Presence filled the room.

"Could you sing some hymns, Mama?" Reinhold begged as the prayers came to a close.

"I'll try." Her voice shaky, Maria sang wistfully the melodies that Reinhold often had requested as a child. The satisfied glow on his face lifted her spirits.

It was already 2 A.M. and Maria's voice was getting raspy. "That is enough," she conceded. "We must all get some sleep—but this has been wonderful!"

The family nodded their heads enthusiastically. "Will you wake me at five, Mama? Maybe Papa and I could visit Kurt at the hospital before I get on the train."

Five o'clock came all too soon, but Maria forced herself from the bed and shook Georg to consciousness. She slipped her robe on and trudged up the stairs to the attic. She shook Reinhold gently and whispered his name. He opened his eyes and rose quickly. Military discipline had tempered him. Returning to the kitchen, Maria took paper and wrapped bread and some sausage for Reinhold to eat. When Reinhold entered the kitchen, his father was waiting for him. Maria let her tears have their way as she put her arms around her son and held him tightly. "God is with you, son," she whispered.

"He is, Mama. I know He is," Reinhold replied, his cheeks shining with his tears.

They parted, and Georg and Reinhold hurried out of the kitchen. Rubbing their eyes and yawning, Ruth and Helmut came stumbling up the stairs. Reinhold ran down to meet them and embraced both at once. With innocent faith, Helmut declared, "We will see you again soon, Reinhold, won't we?"

"I hope you're right, little brother," he replied with a grin.

Fortunately, Georg had brought his ambulance home the previous evening, so he and Reinhold had no trouble getting to the Weissenhof quickly. When they entered Kurt's room, he was still sleeping.

Reinhold tapped his brother's shoulder. Kurt muttered and opened one eye slowly. "Reinhold!" he gasped as he jerked up to a sitting position. "What are you doing here?"

Reinhold smiled and put his arm around him. "It's a long story, and I don't have time to tell you. Ask Papa later." He surveyed Kurt's arm. "You are lucky."

"Lucky? No one ever told me that before! Why?"

"I wish my arm were broken now so I wouldn't have to return to the Russian Front. I'm really afraid."

"Why don't you hide?" Kurt whispered.

"That's too dangerous. Say, tell me about what has happened to your life. Papa told me the good news that God has changed your heart!"

"He is right!" Kurt replied with a grin. "If I hadn't fallen into the Deinenbach with my arm smashed to pieces, I might still be convinced that Hitler is the answer to the world's problems. Now I'm sure that he is the cause of this mess we're in right now. Jesus is the only person who can change the world."

They talked quickly; their time was running out. Tearfully, the brothers held each other, then separated. Catching his regiment could wait no longer.

Let God arise, let his enemies be scattered: let them also that hate him flee before him.

—Psalm 68:1

ten

April 1945

"I WANT TO TAKE YOU AND THE children to Maubach tomorrow morning," Georg announced as he took off his jacket. He had just arrived for lunch, looking very agitated.

Maria turned toward him, dazed with surprise. "You are joking, yes?"

"Of course not! Is this any time to joke, with the Americans' guns so close we can hear them? I have to leave Sontheim in a couple of days. The army has ordered the Red Cross and all security personnel to evacuate. That's why I want you to go; I don't want you living here without me. Dr. Hofherr gave me permission to take you in my ambulance to Christian and Berta's home tonight."

Maria looked puzzled. "Where will *you* go?" She stared at Georg, then glanced at Ruth and Helmut as they sat down at the table.

"I have to haul Nazi records farther south and dispose of them in Lake Constance. I think they contain blacklists of people the Nazis would have punished if they'd won the war. It's almost funny—I'm sure our name is on at least one of those lists! When I finish that job, I hope they'll allow me to return to you." He looked at his wife. "How about it, Maria? Will you go to the Hayers?"

"I would certainly like to. Helmut is so sick from the terror of the war he has already experienced and what lies ahead of him now that it would be good for him to go there. You know that as the bombing has intensified, he has not been

going away from the cellar and won't let me take off his shoes any more because otherwise there isn't enough time to get to the bunker. It is so hard for
him.

"But Berta has her hands full . . . and to take care of more people in her
household, especially in these difficult times when food is scarce, will not be
easy for her either. What should we do?"

"You are right, Maria. I have asked myself the same question. We do not
know how everything will turn out in Maubach either. I am also concerned
about our house and the chickens. What will happen when we are all gone?
Will our home be safe and the chickens fed? We have little time left, and we
have to decide now before it is too late."

"Yes, Georg, these are such difficult and chaotic times. We have to trust the
Lord that we make the right decisions. We will ask Him to direct us."

She turned toward her children. "What do you think, Ruth and Helmut?"

Helmut almost jumped with excitement. "I want to go see Aunt Berta. Please?
I don't like air raids."

Ruth had been sitting quietly and pensively. She stiffened, then blurted, "I
would prefer to come along, but I realize someone needs to look after the
house and the chickens for now. What do you think."

Georg answered first, "Why don't you follow us then with your bike to
Maubach, Ruth."

"I will do that. God has protected me so far, and He will take care of me. I
will look after the house and the chickens. I also know that I can go to the Lenz
family on Staufenbergstrasse to stay and sleep if I feel that it is too dangerous
to remain in our house; they are much farther away from the smokestack of
the yarn factory Ackermann than we are. It will certainly be a target during the
shelling by the Americans, and I will be much safer there. The Lenz family are
believers like us, and one of their daughters told me that her mother wanted to
help us out."

"Thank you, Ruth. You are such a brave daughter. I know that we can depend on the Lenzes; they are such a wonderful Christian family. This arrange-
ment will also give you a chance to check our house and feed the chickens. I
am relieved now about the decision. But be very careful," Georg replied.

"Georg, have you mentioned this to Kurt yet?" Maria asked.

"Not yet. I check on him practically every night, and I will tell him."

Maria ladled the thin soup into bowls and passed them out. "I'm sorry, but this was all the food I dared to use for this meal." She gave a quick smile. "But let's thank the Lord for what we do have, shall we?" The family bowed their heads as Georg prayed hurriedly.

"I'll be so glad to get away from the noise and the killing," Georg began as he spooned his soup. "This whole city has gone crazy. I just heard that Karl D'Angelo, the Heilbronn police chief, fled the city a few days ago. He tried to go to Worms, but as he crossed the Rhine bridge, an explosion killed him and his driver.

"And with the airplanes attacking every day now, there are so many wounded people that the hospitals don't even have room. Karl and I have to leave the victims at the hospital doors and drive off; otherwise, they won't admit them. And now the planes don't even honor the red crosses on our ambulances—we were almost killed yesterday as we drove outside the city! The world has gone mad, I think!"

Ruth looked up from her food. "I think the Nazis are the craziest ones! I saw Herr W___ and Herr Z___ give the Nazi salute to each other on the street this morning." She shook her head in chagrin. "The way they act, you'd think they were actually winning the war!"

Maria interrupted. "And they act like we 'little people' don't even exist. The Nazis eat white bread, butter, eggs, meat, and drink wine—while we stand in line for hours for a cup of sugar and two fish."

In these difficult times life seemed to be more fleeting than ever. Supper that evening was a nervous affair. Georg and his wife didn't have much time left.

"Maria, I will take you and Helmut at midnight. That's the safest time to travel. Make sure that you have everything ready." Then Georg turned to Ruth, "Here is some money for food and other expenses you might have before you leave for Maubach."

He glanced at his watch. "I must hurry back to work. We'll talk more tonight before we leave." He donned his jacket hurriedly and left the house.

Maria, Ruth, and Helmut had time for one more *Dämmerstündle* while they were still at the table. They were especially attentive to Maria's Bible story that night—even restless Helmut. Each of them prayed. They voiced deep-felt concerns—for one another, for their absent Reinhold, for nearby relatives such as Wilhelm and Paula, for friends and neighbors, and for their country.

But the unutterable concerns of a mother's heart could only be lifted to heaven by the groans of her spirit. These were the loves of Maria's life: the man who cared for her and returned her devotion, and the children who were conceived in her womb and fed at her breast. And the futures of all of them could be controlled by only One.

Midnight came quickly. Helmut was led sleepily from his bed to the ambulance. Georg, Maria, and Ruth loaded the bags in the back. Their farewells were brief, each embracing the other. The darkness veiled their tears.

Ruth sniffed loudly, then spoke. "We're never really apart, are we? Not with Jesus in our hearts!"

Maria took her hand and squeezed it. "Ruth, your faith in God makes this parting easier. And I will keep praying for you and for Kurt who is in the hospital." Georg started the motor and Maria stepped into the vehicle, lifting Helmut in ahead of her. She pulled the door shut, and the van lumbered out into the darkened street. The moon was shining brightly, and years later Helmut still remembered how his father, because of the closeness of the Americans, drove carefully and slowly across a bridge with his headlights off.

The clattering growl of the engine made talk difficult, but Maria's heart spoke clearly.

You have protected us this far, Father. From what we have heard, Reinhold is still all right. But we are losing this war, which means that many soldiers are being killed. Are You going to keep him safe any longer? I don't know where Georg will be or how much danger he will encounter. And Kurt and Ruth—I wish I were young and brave again. Without Your protection, we won't all see each other again; we are at Your mercy, Lord. But thank You that heaven awaits us, no matter what happens.

It was now April 2—Helmut's sixth birthday. He would spend the day in more peaceful surroundings than in Sontheim. Only his mother and aunt and uncle would celebrate with him.

Despite his late-night trip, Helmut woke early that morning. As he began to dress, he stopped abruptly and sniffed. The house was filled with exotic smells. From the first-floor blacksmith shop came the acrid fumes of the coal forge and the strong scent of horses being shod. The pigs and hens in the adjoining barn added to the scent. But most intriguing was the tangy odor of smoked meat and homemade sausage hanging in the cellar.

He hurried downstairs and into the kitchen. Aunt Berta was standing over the stove. On the griddle, eggs and potatoes sizzled. Helmut's eyes grew wide at the sight.

Berta looked up. *"Guten Morgen,* Helmut! Happy birthday! Did you sleep well?" Her smile made her full, ruddy cheeks look even bigger. She was a strong-looking woman who worked hard and faced her lot in life with a vigorous faith. Immediately, Helmut felt secure with her.

Christian, the large and muscular blacksmith, was already at work in the shop below. The clanking of his hammer rang through the floor. He was a quiet man, known more for his excellent repairs than for his conversation.

The little village was delightfully quiet. It seemed almost like paradise to Maria and Helmut after the winter of violence in Sontheim. The meadows around Maubach were regaining their green. Here the sirens were moaning only rarely at night to warn of enemy fighter-bombers. Yet, here, too, were painful signs of war, one of which was the absence of young men, of whom many had been drafted into the army. Christian and Berta prayed and wondered daily about their two sons, Gerhard and Hans, who also had gone to war.

❧

Two days after Georg had brought Maria and Helmut to Maubach, he came to Kurt in the middle of the night and said to him, "Tomorrow morning at eight o'clock our Red Cross and all security personnel have to evacuate Heilbronn. I have time and permission from Dr. Hofherr, my commander, to also take you quickly to Maubach."

"That's fine, Father. I will be ready. I have heard that the hospital will release everyone tomorrow who can still walk home because of the dangerous situation from the advancing American Army," replied Kurt, who knew from his father that his mother and Helmut were already there.

The next morning Georg picked up Kurt, and he noticed that his van was already filled with documents and another man from his unit was with him. They were the already mentioned Nazi records, and they had orders to throw them into Lake Constance. Kurt felt increasingly uneasy after they had left the hospital at Weissenhof, and when they had reached the village of Flein he said to Georg quite convincingly, "Sooner, or later, the Americans will be in Maubach too. Bring me home to Sontheim!"

Kurt understood that it wouldn't be easy for the Hayers to take care of an additional person as Germany fell into chaos with an unknown future, and it would be best to stay at home. Also, Maubach would be occupied as well, just a bit later.

When he arrived at home, Ruth was still there and very happy to see her brother Kurt. She stayed with him in Sontheim, encouraged by his brotherly assistance and support. They then braced themselves for the turbulent days before them.

❧

The American guns were now in range of the Heilbronn area and began pounding the city with their destruction. Aside from stepping out for fresh air and to feed the chickens, Kurt and Ruth spent much of their time in the house. They slept in the cellar at night. The rumble of exploding ammunition had become so commonplace that they hardly noticed it unless a shell hit close enough to catch their attention.

After two days, the explosions subsided. Sensing that the lull might be only temporary, Kurt hurried to the bakery, hoping to buy some bread. His promptness was rewarded. Not only did he reach the bakery early enough to avoid a long line but he also received a loaf of bread; there was never a guarantee of enough for every customer. Once home with the bread, he decided that it would be advantageous to buy some other food as well. He headed out again in search of a store that might still have food available. Not relishing the idea of standing in a long line by himself, he stopped at the home of Walter Weller, another wounded soldier like himself. Walter was eager to go along. Together, they hurried down the street.

Suddenly, several gunshots rang out nearby. The two youths halted and stared about them. They exchanged puzzled glances.

"Let's go see what happened," Kurt suggested. "It sounds like the shots came from near the Matthäuskirche." The two walked briskly toward the church, which was little more than a hundred yards away, and turned a corner. Up ahead in the street loomed a large antitank obstacle made of several rows of large timbers imbedded in the pavement. In front of the barricade lay a corpse, its head soaked with blood. As the two approached the sickening sight, they could read the sign wrapped around the body: "I was shot as a war criminal." It was the body of Taubenberger, the former Nazi branch leader of Sontheim, in front of his own house. He had been replaced by the new Nazi branch leader

Nazi-Parade in Market Square in Heilbronn, led by District leader Drauz, the most powerful and most feared Nazi in Heilbronn. After the War he was condemned to death by a U.S. Military Court as a war criminal and executed.

T___ by now. Perplexed by the matter, the two youths returned to their original errand. Nearby, a man was boarding up the windows of his house.

"What happened to Herr Taubenberger, sir?" Kurt asked.

The man looked down from his ladder and shook his head. His voice was somber. "When he came to the barricade, he saw that the small house of family Kühner, who also have several children, was right next to it. This was a great concern to the Kühners as well as to their neighbors. There was fear that the approaching Americans would drive around the barricade and mow down the Kühners house. Some women were working on the street, so Taubenberger ordered them to take their team of horses and pull the fir logs out of the holes they had made in the cobblestone pavement of the street. Herr Wirth, an accountant at the nearby *Schuhfabrik* (shoe factory) Wolko, had just come from work and supported the removal of the antitank obstacle as well. Then he left to join his wife and his daughter in the main bunker near the Matthäuskirche.

"But then District Leader Drauz came by with his three bodyguards. When he saw what was happening, he was furious. Then he asked whose idea it was. One person at the site said Herr Taubenberger and another Herr Wirth. He had Taubenberger arrested and taken to the city hall." He paused. "A few minutes ago, one of Drauz's bodyguards brought Taubenberger back here and shot him. They almost shot Margarete S___, too, because she had helped with it."

❧

Not until later did Kurt find out the whole story about Herr Wirth as he became Herr Wirth's son-in-law when he married his only daughter, Ruth. They were engaged in Sontheim in 1951. Kurt emigrated to the United States of America later that year. Ruth joined Kurt in the United States in 1953, and they were married that same year in Upstate New York.

❧

But now back to the story of Herr Wirth. After he had joined his wife and ten-year-old daughter, Ruth, in the bunker, he realized that he needed to freshen up and shave at home after spending so much time in the bunker where there was no facility for personal hygiene. He left for home and was fortunately not in the bunker when the bodyguard of Drauz looked for him. It saved his life, because he would also have been executed and shot right away.

After Herr Wirth was found, finally, Drauz was already back in Heilbronn. Herr Wirth was then imprisoned in city hall in Sontheim until Drauz could return for the execution of the sentence. He was kept in a locked cell in the cellar of city hall for one week. Each time the door was unlocked, he thought that they were coming to execute him.

When his wife got permission to visit him shortly after he was imprisoned, she took farewell of him and did not expect to see him again. He gave her his personal belongings, including his wedding ring and his gold pocket watch. However, Drauz never returned to Sontheim because he was preoccupied with the approaching American Army and finally had to flee in order to save his life.

On April 6, 1945, when he was fleeing from Heilbronn with three men from the *Volkssturm* (National Defense Force), he had four people executed for treason on Schweinsbergstrasse because they were exhibiting white sheets on their homes, the sign of surrender. They had done this on the advise of a German officer who was leaving the city with other troops one hour before Drauz came.

Later, Herr Stieglitz, the mayor of Sontheim who was favorably inclined toward Herr Wirth, released him from his imprisonment in city hall and let him go home. Thus, God preserved the Wirth's family and brought Kurt and Ruth together later in life. Frau Wirth did not tell her daughter, Ruth, that her father had been imprisoned, and she could not understand why people in Sontheim stayed clear of them when meeting the two on the sidewalks and streets in Sontheim. They were regarded by others as war criminals as well. Only after his release could they assume a normal life again.

The Wirths were never members of the Nazi Party and were sympathetic to the Jews in Germany. The shoe factory that he worked for, Wolko, was owned and started by Hermann Wolf, a German Jew, who had emigrated to the United States of America before World War II. Herr Wirth was able to keep his job at Wolko and did not have to serve in World War II because he was a 50 percent war disabled veteran of World War I.

However, Gerhard Zirkel, a cousin of Ruth's, was not so lucky as Herr Wirth. He was drafted into the German Army, specifically into an air-defense unit, at the end of the war. He was hardly nineteen years old. Four other young men, along with Gerhard, decided to desert from the unit in a forest near Donauwörth and try to make their way home. They were captured by the German SS and hanged by the neck in the forest. Only with the help of God could Ruth's aunt overcome the shock of this tragic loss of her son. But now back to Kurt and Walter.

❧

Dismayed, they proceeded toward the Lichdi grocery store on Hauptstrasse; they had heard from other people that it was one of the few stores in the town with food still available. When they reached the store, they took their places at the end of the long line. They peered anxiously at the customers leaving the store. Their suspicions were correct; each carried only a small package. It seemed useless to wait an hour for so little food, but survival depended on it.

An angry voice rang out from the store and everyone in line strained their ears to listen. "... and anyone who tries to hinder our cause as Herr Taubenberger

Ackermann Yarn Factory with 260-foot Ackermann smokestack—view from across the Neckar where the American Army was shelling Sontheim and hit the smokestack.

did will also be shot as a traitor! Don't forget it!" In a few seconds, a stout man in a uniform stamped out of the store. It was District Leader Drauz.

Finally in the store, Kurt received his ration—two pounds of flour, a small package of salt, and three sausages. He stared disgustedly at the meager rations, then paid the clerk. As he left the store with Walter, his mind went back to Taubenberger's execution. Kurt was astonished at the insanity of the act— yet it only reflected the chaos that enveloped the entire nation. *Even the Nazis are not loyal to the party,* he thought. *They're all interested in themselves. And to think that I wanted to fight for their "new order."*

By the next day, the guns were within range of Sontheim, and shells began hitting the once-peaceful suburb.

During a lull, Ruth went out for a short walk. Soon, she came running back to the house. "Kurt, I just saw Brigitte, and she wants us to come and stay with her. She seems awfully frightened." Brigitte Ellinger was a good friend of Ruth

Staufenbergstrasse with bakery of Herr Bord on left side, and bordering part of Ackermann Yarn factory is Ackermannstrasse, the street on the right. Around 1940.

and her family, and she owned a small grocery store near the Ziefle home. Her mother had died in January, and now her father was at the front, leaving Brigitte by herself.

Kurt brightened. "Our hens laid some eggs today. I'll bet Brigitte has enough things left in her store so we could bake oatmeal cookies." He fetched the eggs, then hurried with Ruth to the store a block-and-a-half away.

Brigitte was overjoyed to see the pair, but Kurt could think only of food. "I brought a few eggs," he announced. "Do you have any oatmeal and sugar left so we can make oatmeal cookies?"

"We're in luck, Kurt," she replied. "I still have two pounds of oatmeal and a half-pound of sugar." The three scurried into the kitchen and busied themselves with the ingredients.

Just as Ruth began mixing the batter, a loud explosion shook the floor. Wide-eyed, the three youths waited for something else to happen. All they heard were the blasts in the distance. They ran outside to see what had been hit. They looked around, but no buildings seemed to be damaged.

Kurt glanced up at the 260-foot smokestack on the Ackermann yarn factory. "Look!" he pointed with his good arm. "A shell went right through the Ackermann chimney! It looks like it could fall any minute."

Fairly immune to danger at this point, the trio finished the cookies and spent the night at Brigitte's, wondering what they should do. The next morning, they sought refuge farther away. Finally, they found shelter in the Lenz home on Staufenbergstrasse; twenty-four people were already crowded into the cellar. Among them were six couples from the Ziefles' neighborhood—the Krauters, Bauers, Bays, Zähs, D___, and Ingelfingers. Life here would be uncomfortable, at best: they had only garden benches on which to sleep, the upstairs bathroom was dangerous to use because of the increased shelling, and the water supply was becoming scarce.

The greatest problem for the twenty-seven people huddled together in the Lenzes' cellar was food. Someone had to go out each day and find more to eat. By now, only two bakers in Sontheim were still making bread for the general public; Herr Bord on Staufenbergstrasse and Herr Kraft on Hauptstrasse had moved their ovens to their cellars and continued baking as long as they had ingredients. They could not deliver, of course, so customers had to come and pick up their bread.

This created an extra challenge for the group in the Lenz home; of the twenty-three adults, only four men were available to make the trip. But Herr Krauter was too old and weak, and Herr D___ was too cowardly. A short man, he compensated for his lack of stature by bragging that he could shoot down enemy planes with only a rifle. Only Kurt and Herr Ingelfinger were willing and strong enough to bring bread from the bakeries and water from the Deinenbach.

As the group was eating supper the evening on which Kurt and Ruth arrived, Ingelfinger turned to D___ and said, "It's your turn to get food tomorrow." His voice was firm. "I did it today, and you promised to do it tomorrow."

D___ flushed. "I . . . I'm not leaving this house for anything. Do you expect me to go out in those streets and be killed?"

"D___, aren't you ashamed of showing such cowardice in front of all these women?" He glared at the short man. "In that case, I'll get it myself."

Kurt interjected, "Let me go. I'm not afraid."

Ingelfinger flashed an approving glance. "No, Kurt, you just came today and brought some food with you. You go the next day." Kurt nodded. Suddenly, there was a loud crash upstairs, and then the cellar shuddered as a shell exploded nearby. In stunned silence, the people sat wide-eyed for a few moments. Someone came clattering down the stairs—one of the women had been in the bathroom during the explosion. The sight of her racing into the cellar, pulling her clothes back on raised a ripple of nervous giggles in the tension-filled room.

"Let's see what happened, Kurt," Ingelfinger called as he hurried toward the stairs. The two stepped out of the house into the evening twilight. They gawked at their shattered chimney, then at the demolished house on the chicken farm next door that belonged to farmer Schwarz.

"Good grief, that was close!" Kurt gasped. "A few feet less and we might all have been killed."

Ingelfinger scratched his grizzled cheek. "I'll bet some chickens were killed by that shell. There's no one living there right now, and we could use some soup!" The two searched and found two dead hens. They returned to the cellar triumphantly.

Late the next afternoon, Ingelfinger set out to fetch bread and water. "Don't worry if I'm a little late," he assured. "I'm going to stop at my house and look for food, so I'll be a little longer."

"Take good care," the group called as he walked out. D___ sat silently in a corner.

As the evening grew late, the residents of the cellar began puzzling as to when Ingelfinger would come. Finally, they concluded that he had been detained and decided to spend the night in his own house. They all went to sleep anticipating his return.

As the group began to stir the next morning, footsteps on the floor above them sent a wave of excitement through the cellar. Frau Ingelfinger rushed toward the steps to greet her husband.

"Irene!" she gasped. "I thought you were my husband." She backed into the room, as her young neighbor walked in with a solemn expression. Her voice quivering, the older woman asked, "Is—there something wrong?"

"Please sit down, Frau," the woman said softly. Frau Ingelfinger sat on a bench, trembling. "Herr Ingelfinger died early this morning at the Children's Clinic. He was wounded by an explosion."

The widow slumped, her face in her hands, and wailed loudly; several people gathered around trying to console her. Kurt turned and stared at D___ whose turn it had been to make that trip. D___ fidgeted and stared at the wall.

As he had passed the *Staufenbergschule,* Ingelfinger was struck in the leg by an exploding shell. Helpless, he lay in the street and cried out. No one heard him. Late in the night, barely conscious, he was discovered by passersby. He was rushed to the Children's Clinic in Sontheim, but he had lost too much blood. In a few hours, he was dead.

Despite the mourning, they had no time to despair. The food supply was low and the water was gone. The chicken soup had sufficed for the evening's meal, but little was left. Kurt, realizing the immediacy of the problem, snatched up a bucket with his good arm and announced, "Look for me in about an hour. I'll go to the Bord bakery first, and then to the Deinenbach for water." He ran up the steps.

Outside, he heard an airplane and looked up. It was a spotter plane; if he was noticed, the observers might direct artillery fire or fighters to strafe the area. Desperately, he lunged toward a nearby tree and waited for the plane to fly out of sight. As soon as it seemed safe, he dashed down the street toward the bakery. Several times shells hit nearby, but he kept going. Breathless, he ran into the bakery.

"Herr Bord," he gasped, "Herr Ingelfinger was killed on the way here yesterday, so we didn't get any bread. Can you give us two loaves today?

The baker shook his head. "Sorry, but I had no bread left from yesterday. I can sell you only one loaf."

Kurt grimaced. "But we are twenty-six people!"

"I wish I could give you more," the man said with a shrug. "Come back tomorrow; maybe I can do something for you then."

With a sigh, Kurt put the loaf into the pail, laid his money on the counter, and dashed out of the store. As he ran toward the Deinenbach, shells were hitting frequently. Sprinting down the street, he murmured, "Lord, help me to get back safely! The people need this bread." At the creek, he took the bread and stuffed it inside his sling. After filling the bucket, he trotted across the field as fast as he could without spilling the water.

As he neared the Lenzes' house, the bucket seemed unbearably heavy. For a moment, Kurt set it down and flexed his arm. Close behind him a shell exploded. He swung his arm down to retrieve the bucket and bolted toward the house.

When he entered the basement, the group greeted him excitedly. Kurt set the bucket on a small table and stopped to catch his breath. Finally, he pulled out the solitary loaf. "I'm sorry, but this was all Herr Bord could spare us." There was a chorus of groans. Kurt tried to sound as cheerful as possible. "I may be able to get more tomorrow; we'll just have to do with less today. Let's be thankful for the food that we still have."

"But the children are crying, and we are all hungry," a woman moaned.

Kurt nodded seriously. "I know. My stomach is growling too." He thought for a few seconds, then beamed. "We will pray!" he exclaimed. The people stared cynically. "Come. Everybody kneel where you are, and I will ask the Lord to help us. He gave the Israelites food in the wilderness, so why can't He give us bread? And if He doesn't give us food, He will certainly help us to get by without it!" The people relented and knelt on the floor while Kurt prayed. A sense of peace and contentment seemed to enter the crowded cellar.

The next day, Kurt ventured to the baker again. Herr Bord seemed much friendlier that afternoon. The group in the cellar was elated when Kurt returned with two loaves of bread. It was now Saturday, April 7, Kurt and Ruth's third night in Lenzes' cellar. Outside, the explosions increased in frequency. Even the unbelievers in the cellar began to whisper prayers for protection.

As the American guns pounded Heilbronn and its suburbs, the Wehrmacht prepared itself for retreat. On Saturday night, the soldiers blew up the footbridge over the Neckar connecting Sontheim and Böckingen. The following night, the people in the cellar were awakened suddenly as the earth shivered with the impact of a huge explosion. The Wehrmacht had just destroyed eight train cars filled with German ammunition.

The next morning, Kurt walked to his home to check for damage. The streets were strewn with plaster, roofing tiles, glass, and wires. Few houses had been spared by the blast. The roof of the Ziefle's house had been jarred loose, and the stone wall in front of the house had shifted. But the damage was minimal in contrast to that of some of the other houses closer to the explosion.

The battle intensified in the following days. The fight for Heilbronn became so violent that it was later referred to as "Little Stalingrad." Mortars, shells, and grenades pummeled the streets and houses incessantly. Night after night, fires broke out, but all major fire-fighting equipment had already been removed from the area. It seemed evident that the Nazi forces could not hold out much longer.

As Kurt ran toward the bakery on the following Wednesday, he came upon a pile of German army rifles alongside Staufenbergstrasse; a strange sense of elation rose inside of him. "The Americans are here—it's all over," he said aloud.

During the night, American troops used boats to cross the Neckar River about two miles southwest of Sontheim. On the north, Heilbronn's defenses crumbled. The group sat helplessly in the cellar, listening to the sounds of combat—the crack and thump of rifles and grenade, and the clanking growl of tanks. As Thursday wore on, it was obvious that Sontheim had been overrun by the Americans. During the night, the shooting stopped.

The residents of the cellar slept little. The morning held only foreboding mystery. Kurt and Ruth did their best to calm the people, but faith came hard for those who had entrusted their future to the Thousand-Year Reich.

About nine o'clock in the morning, two green-clad American soldiers entered the cellar cautiously. Fortunately, Kurt had not worn his Air Force uniform since his accident. Satisfied that no German soldiers were in the house, the Americans departed. To the amazement of the occupants, the soldiers had been very friendly. The attitude of such gracious conquerors quelled much of their fear. There would be curfews and other restrictions, and shortages would still persist; but now they could return to their homes in safety.

❧

In Maubach, things were still somewhat peaceful. Sometimes enemy planes flew over, but they were always heading somewhere else. One now heard of cannons and bombs only on the radio. Only when the body of a fallen son arrived did war again become a harsh reality.

Maria and Helmut walked slowly around the little farming neighborhood as the sun was disappearing. Her phlebitis made walking painful, but Maria needed the time to think. Helmut skipped and ran about, chasing bugs and discovering the spring flowers. She smiled at his antics.

"Mama! May I save these and give them to Ruth?" he asked, holding up a brightly colored bunch.

Maria had not heard anything from Ruth and Kurt since she had left Sontheim, and now even her staunch faith seemed battered and wobbly. But she dared not unveil her fears to her little one. She bit her lip and nodded to him. He suddenly halted his antics, seeming to sense his mother's seriousness. "I wish Papa were here," he said. "Will he come soon?"

Maria groped for confidence. "I'm sure he will come home soon, Helmut, don't worry."

Dear God, don't let me lie to my son.

Bombed-out Heilbronn had almost become a ghost town. Even its landmark, the Kilianskirche (Church of St. Kilian), showed how extensive the damage was from the war.

And shall not God avenge his own elect, which cry day and night unto him, though he bear long with them? I tell you that he will avenge them speedily.

—Luke 18:7–8

eleven

Middle of April 1945

"HERR AND FRAU SCHIELE! When did you arrive here in Maubach?" Maria had last seen the couple in Sontheim where they had taken refuge in a home near the Ziefles' after fleeing from the Red Army advance on Eastern Germany. To Maria's surprise, they now were walking past the Hayers' house in Maubach.

"We are just passing through on our way south," replied Herr Schiele tiredly. "We never expected to be on the road so soon again, but the Americans are closing in."

Maria leaped at the chance to find out about her family. "Have you seen or heard from my children, Kurt and Ruth?" she asked anxiously. "They stayed behind when I came here."

Schiele hesitated before answering. "I haven't been in contact with them, but . . . everything near the Ackermann factory was destroyed when the *Wehrmacht* blew up some ammunition cars. I'm very sorry.

Maria cupped her hand over her mouth and trembled.

"Are . . . are you sure?"

"I saw the wreckage myself."

Maria turned her head away as her composure dissolved. Suddenly, she felt weak. "Excuse me, I must go inside," she murmured and hurried toward the door. The Schieles walked on.

Feeling faint, Maria slumped into a chair. Seeing the distress in his mother's face, Helmut ran to her and laid his head on her lap, hugging her legs. Mutely, she patted his shoulder, hanging on to her composure for his sake. Fortunately, Helmut's bedtime was near.

Solitude became oppressive as her fears closed in on her. She could not face alone the possibility of such a tragedy. Shoulders heaving with suppressed emotion, she rushed to Berta who was sewing in the living room and collapsed on her shoulder. Between sobs, Maria disclosed the news the Schieles had given. Berta sat helpless and silent. She had always assisted her younger sister in word and deed, but now she, too, thought that Kurt and Ruth were probably dead. All she could do was help Maria to her bedroom and trust that the following day would bring better tidings.

Maria lay on her bed and buried her face in the pillow to muffle her sobs from sleeping Helmut. *God, have You betrayed me? Has my family finally been destroyed? It seems impossible, but I don't want to hide from the truth. Please, somehow show me if they are dead or alive.*

The next morning was Sunday. Maria sat silently at her breakfast. If she only could know for sure, it would ease somewhat the terrible burden. There was something horribly cruel in having to *assume* that your children are dead. The complete truth, although tragic, would have been so much less painful and frustrating than presumption.

The family finished eating and began to clean up. Christian left to search for Stefan, his Polish laborer, a war prisoner who had not reported for work in two days. Only a few minutes later, there was a loud knocking at the door. Helmut ran downstairs and opened it. He found himself peering up at a tall Prussian army captain.

"Show me your identity cards," he demanded gruffly as Maria and Berta appeared. The women anxiously hurried to their rooms, then returned with their documents.

The officer examined the documents. Without looking up, he grunted, "Aha! Frau Ziefle, you are not from Maubach. Correct?"

Puzzled, she replied, "That is right."

"I have orders to draft all dispensable individuals immediately, to defend the Fatherland. Because you are only a guest in this house, you must come with me. We will teach you how to use a gun or an antitank weapon."

"Sir! I have a six-year-old son who needs his mother!"

The officer glared at her. "For the Fatherland no sacrifice is too great! If you do not come immediately, I will have you executed as a traitor!"

Maria glanced at Helmut. He stood frozen with fear, obviously understanding to some degree what was happening. Suddenly, he began to cry loudly.

"Shut up, boy!" the man snapped. But Helmut persisted.

Berta could not restrain herself any longer. "Sir, I need my sister—there is too much work in this household for me to do alone. Besides, she has phlebitis—she could not take the strain of combat."

"Every second that the enemy is delayed helps our defenses!" The officer was furious. "A life means nothing if it cannot be sacrificed for Deutschland!"

"Please, sir! I beg you to leave my sister here! I need her!"

The man gave Berta a strange stare. Without another word, he angrily stomped past the women and began searching through the house for deserters. In a few moments, he stalked out, slamming the door behind him. He would search every house in Maubach before he was satisfied.

Maria and Berta stared at each other, puzzled. "I don't know why he changed his mind so suddenly," Maria said with a faint smile, "but I know it was a miracle! It was almost as if he saw or heard someone in this room whom we weren't aware of." She patted Helmut, who had attached himself tightly to her legs. "Thank the Lord we can still be together!"

Berta turned and headed toward the stairs. "We had better get busy baking some more zwieback, eh? We never know when we'll have to start using it." Maria and Helmut followed.

For several days, the people of Maubach had expected that the Americans would come soon. Everyone was nervously making preparations. Berta and Maria had busied themselves by baking large quantities of the hard toast and storing it in the cellar in case of a siege or food shortage. They also had plenty of canned meat and sausage. The days ahead were uncertain, but a good stock of food was reassuring. And the activity kept Maria from succumbing to her nagging fears about her family.

Each day, tension in the village increased. Rumors flourished in the uncertainty, and Maria and Berta tried hard not to believe horror stories they heard concerning the advancing American armies. On Thursday morning, the Prussian captain with a handful of his conscripts hastened out of Maubach on a horse-drawn cart. The people supposed that the end was now imminent.

Early that afternoon, Stefan, Christian's farm laborer, returned—but not alone. With him were twenty other Poles who had been captive workers at nearby farms and businesses. With a strange arrogance, they took over Christian's shop and the food cellar. Casting civility aside, they talked and sang raucously, brandishing sharp knives. When the Nazis had invaded Poland, these people had been shipped to Germany as human plunder. For five years they had been virtual slaves. The roles were now being reversed. With the American armies approaching, the Poles flaunted their inevitable freedom, and their German masters were powerless to control their prisoners. Many Eastern laborers would seek revenge against their overseers. Fortunately for Christian and Berta, they had always been kind to Stefan.

The women did not dare to enter the cellar any longer. "There goes all our meat and zwieback," Berta sighed. "All we have left is this one tin of bread in the kitchen."

Maria was staring out the window. "All the farmers are coming back from the fields already," she observed. "Look, Berta! Some of the neighbors are hanging sheets and pillowcases out their windows for white flags! The Americans must be coming!"

Berta paled. "Maria, what will we do? What will they do to us?"

Maria sensed a fresh surge of confidence in her spirit as she approached her sister and put her arm around her. "The Lord knows what will happen. Let's trust Him to pull us through." Berta nodded nervously.

"Let's go outside and find out what is happening," Maria suggested. She turned toward the adjoining room and called, "Helmut! Let's go outside!"

Her son scurried through the door and down the stairs ahead of the women. Christian already had been outside visiting with a neighbor, and he hurried to join them when he saw them step out into the street.

In the street, several people, their faces tense, conversed in small groups. A strange noise caught Maria's attention; in the distance was a muffled, droning growl. She thought back to the dreadful night in December, but this was different—it was not the sound of airplanes.

"We'd better go back into the house," Christian suggested. "We'll probably be safer there." The women and Helmut followed him upstairs. From the living room they could observe the event from an open window. The whole village watched as if a parade were approaching.

In minutes, a long line of dark green trucks, jeeps, and tanks moved through the streets of Maubach. The citizens watched spellbound.

"Mama!" Helmut exclaimed. "There's a man with black skin in that tank!"

"They are called Blacks, Helmut. Many of them live in America." Helmut continued to stare in fascination.

A captain walked toward the house, looking up at the window. "Are you Polish?" he shouted in English. The four at the window looked at each other and shrugged their shoulders.

"Are you Polish?" he shouted louder.

"I think he's asking if we're Poles," Christian suggested. He and Berta and Maria shook their heads at the officer.

"Raus! Raus!" he yelled back. "You have twenty minutes to get out."

The party in the window again shrugged their shoulders and shook their heads; none of them understood the English part of the command. The captain, with improvised sign language, finally made them understand. Quickly, the four grabbed the zwieback from the kitchen, two blankets from a bedroom, then hurried down to the street. They were now refugees.

The family walked along the street toward the public bakeshop, the nearest building. Inside, they found the fire in the oven still burning. "My, isn't this cozy," Christian joked. "Maybe there's some bread in here as well." He looked in the oven; two large, fragrant loaves of farmer's bread were baking. He pulled them out and said, "These should take care of us for at least four days!"

As he spoke, a neighbor girl walked in and picked up her two loaves. Disappointed, Christian dropped down on a bench.

A black soldier wearily tramped into the room. "Raus! Raus!"

"Not again!" Christian shook his head impatiently. The soldier did his best to explain that the German forces that had retreated hastily were planning a counterattack for the evening; the bakeshop would be in the line of fire. Somehow the little group got the message and left. Now they would have to find another place to stay.

"Sorry, our cellar is full." They would try the next house.

"Four people? We don't have that much room left." They trudged on.

"Try Grubers next door; they might be able to help." It was shattering to be turned away by one's own neighbors. The sun was setting.

Desperate, they tried the farmer Sachs. "Frau Sachs," Christian began, "the Americans have forced us out of our house. Could we stay with you?"

"I wish I could help you, Herr Hayer, but we already have too many staying in our cellar."

"We can't sleep in the open tonight!" Christian was disgusted. "How about if we sleep upstairs?"

The woman looked at him astonished. "You want to stay up here when the shooting starts?" She flapped her arm at him. "It's all yours, if you're crazy enough to try it. But we're spending the night in the cellar."

Christian turned to the women and asked in weary desperation, "Well, what should we do?"

Berta answered instantly, "We'll take it—won't we, Maria?"

"We don't have much choice," Maria conceded.

Upstairs, they found two beautiful bedrooms. The eiderdown comforters and clean white bedsheets were much more inviting than a damp, crowded cellar.

"Mama, will we be killed when the battle starts?" Helmut asked innocently.

"No, I don't think so," Maria answered. "The Lord has protected us through this war, and I trust He'll continue to. Let's get you ready for bed." As she undressed him, she called Christian and Berta to join them for a time of prayer.

The four sat on Helmut's bed together. "We must pray for the Lord's protection tonight." They all bowed their heads, and each of them prayed in turn, remembering the family members who were not with them.

As Christian and Berta left for their bedroom, Maria tucked Helmut in. "Sleep well," she said. "God is with us." She kissed him and turned away, her heart crying out, *Lord, this could be a terrible night. If Helmut wakes up, he will be horribly frightened by all the noise. Please, please keep him asleep all night.*

She climbed into her bed.

Within the hour, German artillery unleashed its fury against the American forces in the village. The American gunners immediately returned the fire, filling the air with the screams and blasts of explosive shells. Suddenly, an earsplitting explosion occurred; the Germans had blown up the nearby railroad bridge. Berta and Maria rose from their beds and joined each other in the hallway to pray. Their vigil lasted the whole night.

Christian came into the hall, muttering angrily, "This is insane! Our armies are beaten, so why don't they surrender instead of shooting at their own people?" The women agreed. But the firing did not cease until the sun was ready to rise.

As sunlight began to gleam through the window, Helmut stirred and opened his eyes. He turned and saw his mother sleeping on the other bed. The air was quiet. "We're alive!" he called. "Mama, the Lord kept us alive!"

Maria turned wearily toward her son and smiled in spite of her tiredness. "And He kept you asleep, Helmut. The noise of the guns was terrible, but you never woke up!" She pulled her covers closer. "Play quietly for a little while so that Mama can get some sleep."

Later, Berta came in and awakened her sister. With Christian, they proceeded downstairs. The owners of the house and some of their companions were in the kitchen eating.

"We want to thank you for the use of your house last night," said Christian.

"It was nothing," Frau Sachs replied. "Here, sit down and eat. The least I can do is feed you." Gratefully, the four accepted her invitation.

One of the men spoke. "You are either brave or stupid—we never expected to see you folks alive this morning!"

"It was the Lord who kept us," Maria said seriously. "We spent most of the night praying. I'm glad it's over!"

Berta interrupted. "You'll be very crowded in here now, so I suppose we'll have to find another place to stay."

Frau Sachs replied, "I wish we had room for you. Why don't you try the Schultzes down the street?"

As soon as they finished their meal, they thanked their hosts again, then walked out into the street. The town crier was coming toward them. They stopped to listen to his announcement: the Americans had instituted a twenty-two-hour curfew, from 11:00 A.M. to 9:00 A.M. Fortunately, it was just 9 o'clock, so they had the full two hours to find new lodging.

Tired of this endless search, Christian suggested, "Berta, why don't we check our house? Maybe we could return there."

"I'd rather stay there than in someone else's home," she agreed.

When they reached their house, however, they discovered that the Americans had moved in and set up temporary quarters. Disappointed, they retraced their steps and approached the Schultz family. Herr and Frau Schultz, an elderly couple, were happy to accommodate the four wanderers. They also had gleaned information about the aftermath of the previous night's fighting. A large number of livestock had been killed and some buildings were destroyed. Most saddening, however, were the civilian casualties—several were wounded, and a ten-year-old girl was killed. Maria sensed afresh the pain of not knowing the fate of Kurt, Ruth, and her husband.

Confined by the curfew, the Ziefles and the Hayers spent the rest of the day keeping themselves occupied. The women helped Frau Schultz cook and sew. Christian discussed farming and the war with Herr Schultz for a while, then found a book that intrigued him. Helmut played with the cat.

During the two hours of freedom that day, rumors had multiplied among the residents of Maubach. Especially frightening to Helmut was the claim that if Americans caught children breaking curfew, they would haul them away in trucks, never to be seen again.

The next morning, about 8:30, Helmut stepped out the backdoor to play in the small yard. Just across the fence, an American soldier patrolled the street, enforcing the curfew. His head turned toward Helmut. Helmut dashed into the house and hid behind the door in terror. Nothing happened. Still frightened, though, he spent the rest of the morning close to his mother.

As soon as the curfew had lifted, Berta, Maria, and Helmut walked back to the Hayers' house to find more blankets; the Schultzes' house had been rather cold at night. Maria had brought her best blankets from Heilbronn to Christian and Berta's. Helmut dreaded meeting more soldiers on the street; he was glad to be with his mother.

A soldier with a rifle hanging from his shoulder barred entrance to the house. Helmut timidly clutched his mother's dress. "Sir, this is my sister's house," Maria said slowly, hoping the man would understand. "We would like to go in and get some blankets we left behind—we were forced to leave on sudden notice."

The guard stared blankly. "Captain," he finally answered.

Not sure what he meant, the trio stepped toward the door. The soldier maneuvered to stay in front of them. "Captain," he said again, but they kept moving closer. He raised his voice. "Captain! Captain! Captain!" But the language barrier was too great. Frantically, he pulled the rifle from his shoulder and pointed it toward them.

"Mama! Please, don't go any farther!" Helmut cried out, pulling at his mother's arm. She stopped.

"Captain!" the man said loudly, pointing his finger toward a building down the street. Finally, they understood and went to find his superior. Fortunately, the captain could speak some German, and he gave permission to enter the house.

Maria went in alone. When she reached the top of the stairs and entered the living quarters, she gasped in horror. Drawers and closets had been emptied, and the contents were littered all over the floor. Five large, unshaven soldiers were sprawled on the two sofas and armchairs. She sensed their discomfiting stares. Maria quickly moved to the hutch, pulled out the four blankets, and hurried down the steps, retreating from the unnerving eyes.

An hour still remained before the curfew began, so the three decided to check the Hayers' garden plot just outside the village. As they walked toward the garden, they came to a spot that afforded a clear view of the highway. They were overwhelmed by the sight. A seemingly endless column of trucks and jeeps rumbled toward Stuttgart; they had never seen so much military equipment.

"Mama, may I stay here and watch the cars and trucks while you look at the garden?" Helmut begged.

Maria and Berta glanced at each other hesitantly. "If you promise to stay right here and not move," Maria finally agreed. Helmut nodded eagerly.

The two women went on to the garden. To their relief, they found it had been unharmed by the shelling two nights earlier. They spent some time pulling weeds and enjoying the fresh air. Soon the curfew was almost upon them, and they hurried to retrieve Helmut and go home.

When they reached Helmut, the line of vehicles was still passing with no sign of its ending. Maria wondered at the sight: what kind of nation is this that has so much military might? It seemed ridiculous that Germany had even attempted to fight such an army.

They walked home briskly, not wanting to be caught on the streets after 11:00. At home, they were greeted by Christian with the good news that the curfew had been lifted, except for night hours. He had also heard that in about a week the Americans would vacate houses that they had commandeered.

Maria's heart leaped at the news. Could it be that the war was almost over? It was as if her soul had been released after six years of imprisonment. The godless Reich had been crushed. She wept silently. She did not know where her husband was, her eldest was at the Russian Front, and her second son and her only daughter were possibly dead; yet she was finally free. No more "Heil Hitler," no more persecution of innocent people, and no more bombings. Germany was again at peace.

The soldiers who spoke the strange language were not overly friendly to the Germans yet. After a long bloody war, they could not help but be suspicious of the people who were seemingly responsible for oppressing and killing so many millions of people.

But Helmut was fascinated by the invaders. Most enticing to him was the food that these soldiers ate. He had experienced hunger for as long as he could remember, and here were people who had all they could eat and more. Deliberately, he would stand close to the cooks' tent, hoping for a handout. His eyes nearly popped out when he saw scrambled eggs filling a pan so big that he could have lain down in it; he had never seen so much bread as he did the day that two trucks, bulging with loaves, pulled up to be unloaded.

But all of this abundance was denied the local citizens. Painfully, they endured the humiliation of defeat and their loss of rights.

Finally, the Hayers and the Ziefles were allowed to move back to their house. Maria had warned Christian and Berta about the mess that she had seen inside; but after a week, it was even worse. Berta cried out with horror at the sight. Clothing, books, utensils and important papers were strewn everywhere. A quick check revealed that the soldiers had taken only items that they considered souvenirs of the Nazi era. The family set about to restore order.

Maria had become increasingly concerned to find out the truth about Kurt and Ruth, and she wanted to return to Sontheim and discover it for herself. But she had no idea how to make the trip. The open countryside was still not secured completely by the Americans; also, many resentful Eastern Europeans who had been POWs were staying out in the country, making travel risky.

Finally, she approached the American captain and asked his advice. He suggested that she go to the nearby village of Backnang and secure permission from his commander to go to Sontheim. The biggest obstacle in the trek to Backnang turned out to be Helmut. They both were fearful as they left the relative safety of Maubach. When they walked past the last houses of Maubach and faced the open fields, Helmut panicked and began to cry. "I won't go," he insisted as tears rained down his cheeks.

"Don't be scared, Helmut," Maria assured. "I'm going with you."

"No, we'll be shot! I just know we will."

Maria tried to pull him along, but he resisted, stamping his feet and crying even louder. She had never seen her son so stubborn. Finally, she picked him up and spanked him soundly. Whimpering, he followed grudgingly.

The trip was a waste of time. The commander refused to allow a woman and child to travel alone. Crushed, Maria and Helmut trudged homeward. She was glad that Helmut was too busy observing his surroundings to notice her tears. Silently, she pleaded, *What am I to do, Lord? I need to know the truth about my children. Please make a way for me.*

Discouragement drained her last reserves of strength as she walked.

Finally they reached Maubach and turned down the street to the Hayer home. A shout caught her attention. "Mama! Mama!" She eyed the house. Someone was waving an arm wildly from a second-story window. Then she saw the other arm hanging still—in a large white cast.

"It's Kurt!" Helmut yelled, and he dashed ahead of his mother. Fresh energy surged through her and she quickened her pace. "Thank you, Lord, for answering my prayers!" Maria said aloud as she neared the door. She hurried up the stairs and tearfully gathered Kurt in her arms. "God is so good!" she cried out.

She stepped back and looked him over. "What about Ruth?"

"Oh, she's fine. She can't wait to see you!"

"You don't know how much this means, Kurt! I've just tried to secure permission for traveling to Sontheim, but the commander denied it because it was too risky. I had to find out the truth because some people from Sontheim told me that everything near the Ackermann factory was destroyed—and that you were probably dead." She hugged him again. "I can hardly believe this is happening!"

"Those people were mistaken," Kurt assured her. "Our house is still standing, although the roof was knocked loose by an explosion. But I've already fixed it. And the factory was only partially damaged."

"Have you heard anything from Papa?" Maria asked eagerly.

Kurt's expression became serious. "No. And Berta told me you don't know about him either. We'll have to keep praying for him as well as for Reinhold."

"Mama, how about leaving for home tomorrow morning? Ruth is expecting us."

"The sooner the better," Maria replied. "But how did you come here? By bicycle?"

"It wasn't easy with my cast, but I rode all the way."

Berta and Christian preferred that the Ziefles wait until the countryside was safer, but they understood their longing to be reunited in their own house. In the morning, Berta fed them a hearty breakfast and supplied them with boiled eggs and sandwiches to eat on the way. After a short time of prayer together, the three set out on a seemingly endless thirty-mile trip.

Kurt's bicycle was so loaded with luggage that no one could ride it. It was difficult to push it with only one arm, but he took over his task valiantly, Maria helping to steady the bike. Thankfully, the weather was beautiful.

The route, although flanked by spring's bright fresh colors, was marred by the remnants of war. There were countless antitank obstacles; the roads were pocked with shell craters; blown-up bridges lay twisted in the streams; many fields bore scars from the ravages of artillery; and abandoned German tanks, trucks, and mobile artillery stood in ghostly silence.

Helmut kept up with the two adults bravely; they walked as fast as possible to reach home before the evening. Every few miles, they stopped to rest, but only for a few minutes. At Grossbottwar, about twelve miles from Sontheim, they were extremely thirsty and searched until they found a farmer who would give them milk. Refreshed, they went on.

About four miles from home, Helmut pleaded, "Can't we sit down? I'm too tired to walk anymore." They stopped and let him rest.

Kurt grinned at his brother. "A soldier in Sontheim gave me a chocolate bar, Helmut. If you'll be brave and walk all the way home, I'll give it to you!"

Helmut leaped to his feet, exclaiming, "Chocolate!" He puffed out his little chest and set his face resolutely. "I'm going to make it anyway, chocolate or no chocolate!"

"That's the spirit!" Kurt replied, tousling Helmut's hair.

It was after four o'clock as they approached Sontheim. When they were less than a quarter-mile from the first house, the rhythm of their footsteps was suddenly interrupted by the "thwang!" of rifle bullets hitting the field next to them. Kurt dropped the bike and pulled Helmut and Maria to the ground.

"This is ridiculous!" he muttered. "We come all this way without trouble, then die in sight of our town!" He looked around. Americans had shot at them— apparently for no reason at all—from a moving truck.

The shooting subsided; after waiting a while, the three Ziefles stood slowly and brushed themselves off. Kurt picked up the bike and started moving. "Let's go as fast as we can!" he ordered. "They might start shooting again." Summoning all of their energy, they hurried toward the town, all three pushing the bicycle together. As they reached the shelter of the houses, they slowed their pace, their hearts pounding and lungs aching.

Finally at their own house, Maria and Helmut rushed up the stairs to see Ruth. "We're home, Ruth!" Helmut shrieked, running ahead of his mother.

There she stood at the head of the stairs, smiling and holding out her arms. The three embraced eagerly.

Ruth had already cooked supper for them, but Maria collapsed on the sofa and rested her aching legs and feet. Although she had not complained, the last half of the trip had been agony for her. Kurt and Helmut joined her. Their couch had never felt so good. It had been more than three weeks since Maria and Helmut had left.

"Well, before we eat, we must thank God for reuniting us," Maria announced. The others knelt with her beside the sofa. "And we must pray especially for Papa and Reinhold."

They had hardly finished praying when a clattering noise on the street caught their attention. Kurt went to the window and looked. "There's a strange man coming up to our house."

The others joined him at the window. A man pushing a rickety baby carriage was approaching their door. He was unshaven, and on his ragged jacket was a large white *P.*

"He must be a Pole," Maria said quietly. "I'll go see what he wants." She went downstairs and opened the door.

Their eyes met, and the two people stood speechless for a moment. "Georg!" Maria cried as they hugged each other. "We didn't know if you were dead or alive!"

Georg straightened up and grinned at his wife. "It's obvious I'm not dead!" The children dashed down the stairs to greet their father; gleefully they gathered around him.

As they ushered him upstairs to the dining room, he began telling his story. "I dumped the files I was hauling at the town of Constance in Lake Constance. Then my unit went to Sigmaringen to stay until we received further orders. However, the Americans arrived soon. I had left my ambulance in the barn of a farmer. When the Americans searched the house I was hiding in the rest room. Yet, when I came out they noticed that I was still wearing the pants of my uniform. An American soldier told me, "Stay in the house until we pick you up!" He was very nice to me and also gave me a chocolate bar after I helped him repair a radio. But when no one showed up the next day to pick me up, I got lost. The farmer gave me a Polish jacket and a baby carriage. Then I walked from Sigmaringen to Maubach and wanted to bring you back to Sontheim. Oh—I almost forgot!" He reached into his pocket and pulled out a chocolate bar. "I want you to have it, Helmut."

Helmut's eyes grew big. "Two chocolate bars in one day! This is better than a birthday!"

Georg continued. "I walked to Maubach to find you and arrived two hours after you left. I had brought the baby carriage in case Helmut became tired of walking. Anyway, Berta told me about your stay with her and about Kurt's coming to bring you home. As soon as she had fed me, I came to Sontheim as fast as I could."

"But why are you wearing that awful jacket? Isn't it for Polish prisoners?" Kurt asked.

Georg laughed. "With the Americans imprisoning Nazis, and many Poles acting like bandits, it's a lot safer right now to travel as a Pole."

"I'm just glad we're all safe," Maria concluded. "Tonight we can all go to bed early and get some rest. This house is going to need much fixing tomorrow." Maria's eyes welled up. "My only wish is that Reinhold were here with us."

Never again lamentations, war, betrayal and dire times! No child that screams at night in terror because of the beating of boots on the pavement.
—Jürgen Henkys

twelve

May 1945

GEORG ZIEFLE WALKED SLOWLY through the gate and into his yard, his shoulders drooping. He halted and looked nervously around at his family. Maria and Ruth were hanging laundry; Kurt and Helmut were chopping wood for the stove. Ruth turned her head and saw her father. "Any letters, Papa?" she inquired eagerly.

Georg walked closer and his hands trembled as he drew an envelope from his shirt pocket. "Come here—all of you." His voice was strained. The others soberly gathered around him as he took a sheet of paper from the envelope and held it before them. "This is from the government. Reinhold was captured by the Russian army last month and is a prisoner of war."

Maria gasped, her hand over her mouth. She snatched the letter from her husband's hand to read it for herself.

Georg stared woodenly ahead as he explained, "According to the letter, he was captured in the Spreeforest while retreating after the fall of Berlin." He hesitated, and his voice dropped. "I am afraid for his safety; I've been told the Russians can be very cruel. We must face the fact that we may never see him again."

"No," Maria said firmly although her face was already streaked with tears. "He will not die. I cannot believe that the Lord has brought our family safely this far only to allow Reinhold to die. These are hard days, but we will be together again—I am sure."

Kurt spoke solemnly. "I don't have as much faith as Mama, but I think she is right. I think if we pray, God will keep our brother." Then, with a wry grin, he added, "Maybe an angel will take him out, just like Saint Peter in the Bible!" Their faces softened at his remark.

"Maria, you pray right now," Georg suggested. She nodded and the others bowed their heads.

Maria's voice trembled as she began. "I thank You, God, that You know our sorrows. You have watched over us through this war and have kept us all alive—thank You for miracles. But now again we are helpless. Please take good care of Reinhold, wherever he is—we want to have him with us again. Cause his captors to be merciful." Her voice caught. "We also know, Lord, that You did not keep Your Son from death. So we say, as Jesus said before He was arrested, 'Not my will, but thine, be done.' Amen."

The family chorused in low voices, "Amen."

"I will go make some lunch," Maria announced matter-of-factly. The rest of the family returned to their work until she called them for lunch.

Making lunch was more easily said than done. Those first weeks after the war had been brutally harsh. All utilities were still inoperative. Water had to be carried from the Deinenbach; light came from only the wood stove and the one skinny candle rationed to them each week at the city hall.

Finding food was the main struggle. The family was allowed one loaf of bread each week, in addition to what little else might be available. The Ziefles took turns standing in long lines to receive bread, a small measure of oatmeal, or a quart of watery, bluish milk. In marked contrast, the American forces that had set up headquarters in the Ackermann facilities only a block from the Ziefle home enjoyed a variety and abundance of food.

Fortunately, it was springtime, and the Ziefles would soon have food from their garden. Their dozen hens supplemented their diet with eggs.

None of the family was able to find employment yet, so each member was busy with the task of survival. Working in the garden, chopping firewood, and collecting grass and other food for the chickens not only provided necessary food and heat but also kept each person occupied both physically and mentally.

Food shortages and other hardships, though, were mere inconveniences to the Ziefles and other Germans in contrast to the lawlessness of the vengeful Poles and other Eastern Europeans who now roamed through the city and countryside. The Allies had provided food and housing for many of them at the old military barracks in Heilbronn, but now, free from German oppression, they wanted no restrictions.

Unlike the German citizenry, the East Europeans were not under travel restrictions. And because they were not under close scrutiny, many of them carried weapons.

Some of these foreigners broke into homes in broad daylight, robbing and terrorizing the German families. They butchered livestock at will, gorging themselves on the meat. A German attempting to stop them was taking his life into his own hands. One local farmer tried to prevent two Poles from picking his cherries and was brutally murdered with his own sickle.

Georg straightened up and looked happily at the season's first three gladiolas he had just picked; Maria would be delighted. Soon the dozens of green stalks around him would be exploding with color.

"How much for those flowers?" said a voice gruffly. Georg turned to see two Poles approaching him from behind. He did not want to part with them, so he suggested an absurd price: "Three marks."

One of the men reached into his jacket pocket and pulled out a knife, deftly flicking it open. He pointed the blade at Georg's stomach and glared icily. "Give them to me."

Georg glanced down at the menacing blade. He had heard enough reports to know that these men would not hesitate to kill him, even for three flowers. His heart pounding, he quickly handed them to the man. The pair turned toward each other and laughed, then sauntered away.

Dejected, Georg went home and told Maria about the incident. She was horrified at the thought of losing her husband over flowers.

We thought the danger was over when the war was finished, Lord. Now we live in danger of being murdered by these lawless thugs. Change their hearts and protect us.

A political struggle for survival also began among the formerly adamant Nazis. As soon as Germany had surrendered, those who had harassed and sometimes brutalized the Germans who refused to cooperate with the Nazi cause became strangely docile and benevolent. The Ziefles found it strange to see people who shortly before had scoffed at religious faith suddenly sitting in the front pews of the church, attentively absorbing Pastor Brendle's sermons. Fearing that the victims of their persecution would lodge complaints and have

them arrested, they hoped that their newfound piety would move the courts
to be lenient toward them. Some of them also hoped to get an exoneration
certificate from the pastor. The Ziefles were also baffled when neighbors who
had treated them so coldly during the war now greeted them with dramatic
warmth. Maria could not help feeling a sense of justice as she saw some of
these people taken away for questioning by the new authorities. But from the
bottom of her heart she wished for them profound transformations. These,
too, one could experience.

Just as remarkable was the about face in the editorial viewpoint of the local
newspaper, the *Heilbronner Stimme.* Preceding the fall of the Third Reich, the
paper had pleaded for the citizens to give a superhuman effort in defense of
the Fatherland. They had quoted the Führer's words as if they were divine
proclamations.

In the first issue after the surrender, however, the *Stimme* bore the headline,
"No More War for Ninety-nine Years." The editorial that followed suggested
that Germany ban and never again manufacture any type of weapon—
including knives. This sharp attack on war and weaponry and the strong
support for a peaceful society almost had biblical overtones.

*I am puzzled, perplexed, by this sudden blossoming of civility. How can men
be hateful and barbaric, then suddenly become virtuous and gentle? I know, Lord,
that You can change hearts—You did it for Kurt—but I do not hear any talk of
God from these people. I wish that what I have seen on the outside would reflect
a change on the inside; show them that their own righteousness is only filthy rags
without the real change that only Your Spirit can bring.*

Each day, one of the Ziefles hurried to the post office, longing to receive
some news from Reinhold. When mail delivery was finally restored, the family
waited eagerly each day for the postman to come through their neighborhood.
They still did not know even where he was interned; any mail they sent was
routed through a central Russian military address. They had sent Reinhold
two packages of food that they were able to spare.

One morning late in the summer, Kurt and Helmut were playing ball in the
yard when they saw the postman approaching. "I'll race you!" Helmut chal-
lenged his brother as he began running toward the man. Kurt purposely allowed his little brother to take the lead and receive the delivery. Helmut, puffing,
turned toward Kurt with a letter clutched in his hand. "Look, Kurt!" He turned
the envelope toward him so he could read it. "Where is it from?"

Kurt studied the stampings on the paper. "It's from eastern Germany. I'll bet it's from Reinhold! Let's take it up to Mama and Papa." The two scrambled into the house and up the stairs.

With trembling fingers, Georg Ziefle ripped open the envelope. Nervously, he pulled out the thin gray paper, then glanced at the signature. "This is from Reinhold!"

Most of the letter had been defaced with heavy black marks—censoring by prison officials. All that was left was the assurance that Reinhold was in good health and that he was temporarily in eastern Germany. He also noted that only one prisoner, someone named Ochs from Karlsruhe, a town near Heilbronn, had received any packages.

"That means that the two packages we sent never reached him," said Kurt sadly. "I wish there were some way to be sure that we could get a package to him."

Maria, her faith reassured, said, "We will pray, and the Lord will make a way."

The news about the packages was a disappointment, but it could not dampen their delight at having heard from Reinhold. Their hopes for his return were for the moment raised high. However, the abundance of the black censoring struck a note of concern in Maria's heart.

There are things we do not know, things that are being concealed from us. If his captors are so eager to hide information from us, what are they doing to my son? Are they giving him enough food? Are they beating him? Strengthen my son, O Lord. I do not want to lose him now.

❧

The return to a normal life came slowly for the Germans. The people were attempting to recover not only politically and economically but also physically and spiritually. With help from the Americans, services were restored gradually, and many Germans were busy repairing and rebuilding their bomb-gutted cities. Georg Ziefle's experience as a salesman and as an ambulance driver didn't conform to the need of the moment for skilled journeymen and laborers. Nonetheless, Georg kept himself occupied as he and Kurt, somewhat hampered by his slow-healing arm, repaired their house and helped many neighbors to clean up and fix their property.

Georg was supposed to get a job with the Public Health Office in Heilbronn and a reward of twelve hundred German Reichsmarks if he could bring his Red Cross car from Sigmaringen, where it was still in the barn of the farmer, to Heilbronn. Sigmaringen was now under French control in the French Occupation Zone. Georg took along a car battery because the old one had already been weak when he left the car there. When he arrived in Sigmaringen, all four tires were flat and he had to drive to Heilbronn on the rims. There he delivered the car and was hired by the Public Health Office; however, for some unknown reason, he did not get the reward money. At the Public Health Office, Dr. Graner appointed him for the control of epidemics to test the water wells for all ninety-nine communities in the rural district of Heilbronn and determine if the drinking water was safe for consumption.

Even before Georg found employment, Kurt had acquired an apprentice-ship in Heilbronn at the Ritzmann photography studio. He found the trade much to his liking and excelled in the field.

Ruth had resumed her studies in chemistry. She was looking forward to soon working as a laboratory assistant in the Vogelman chemical firm.

Helmut began first grade at the Bauschool in Sontheim. Even pencils and paper were in short supply, so the students practiced their writing skills on small blackboards that they carried to class each day. Despite the difficulties, he attacked the adventure of learning with relish.

৯৵৽

Reinhold had now been a prisoner for more than a year. He had been able to send one more letter to his family, informing them of his internment in a camp in Poland. The profusion of black ink across the lines of the letter increased his family's suspicions that things were not pleasant for him. They longed to be able to see him, or at least to send him something that would encourage and strengthen him.

The opportunity finally came during that summer of 1946. With delight, Maria received a letter informing the family that a care package from the United States had arrived for them. They could claim it at the relief center in Neckargartach, a northwestern suburb. "It must be from my sister Emma, in New York," Maria concluded. Without delay, Maria, Ruth, and Helmut hurried off to claim their package. They took along the old baby carriage in which to carry the package in case it was heavy. Streetcar service had been restored partially, so they were able to ride most of the distance.

Upon arriving at the relief center and receiving the package, they were glad to have brought the cumbersome carriage. The package was not only heavy but also bulky. It was addressed from Emma and her husband, Reinhold. They hurried home with their prize to open it with the rest of the family. By the time they arrived, Kurt and Georg were both home from work. Excitedly, they began to open the box, which in itself was no small task; the package had been well sealed, and each item inside was wrapped and tightly packed. It was a glorious gift: candies, chocolate bars, chewing gum, and cans of cheese and sausage left them staring wide-eyed. Maria handed each person a small sample of chocolate. They accompanied their eating with enthusiastic "M-m-ms" and "Ah-h-hs."

As they reveled in their newfound treasure, Maria suggested, "Let's save the best items and send them to Reinhold. I have a feeling that he's going through difficult times and needs these things much more than we do."

"But how will we send it if the other two packages never reached him?" Georg questioned.

"I have been thinking about that," Maria replied, "and I may have a solution. Reinhold wrote that a prisoner named Ochs from Karlsruhe did receive some packages. Since Karlsruhe is nearby, why don't we have his family send the gift for us?"

"That, Maria, is a wonderful idea!" Georg replied with admiration. "But who will go to Karlsruhe? Kurt and I can't get away from our jobs."

"I'll go!" offered Ruth. So the next morning, with a carefully wrapped package in her arms, she boarded the train for Karlsruhe.

In her youthful lightheartedness, she did not think that it would be very hard to locate the Ochs family. Not far from Karlsruhe, the train stopped on the open track. "Everyone get out! *Terminus!*" the ticket inspector called. Ruth did not know that the train did not drive all the way to Karlsruhe because of a railroad bridge that had been blown up. What now? She set out to look for a post office or a police station where someone might be able to help her. She had taken only a few steps when she heard how two men greeted each other. "Good morning, Herr Ochs!" said one of them and took off his hat. Ruth stood rooted to the spot. Had she already reached the destination of her trip? She pulled herself together and asked Herr Ochs if he had a son who was a prisoner of war in Poland.

"No," he replied, "but the son of my sister-in-law is in Poland. Perhaps you will find something there. But she lives still almost fifteen miles from here." He named the place and walked on. Ruth stood undecidedly and wondered how she could get there. Suddenly, Herr Ochs turned around and came back. Glancing at his watch he said, "Down there is the post office. From there, a bus that will stop directly in front of the house of my sister-in-law will leave in five minutes. Then it turns around and returns to here."

Ruth believed that she was dreaming when she found everything as Herr Ochs had described for her. Frau Ochs was very friendly and offered that the Ziefles could send their packages to her, and she would forward them to Reinhold.

When Ruth talked about her experiences at home, the whole family was astonished at how God's hand was in all of these events and how it had turned out so wonderfully. They were thankful that now they could support Reinhold a little with provisions. They had no idea how sorely he needed the packages. Reinhold each day lived in the shadow of death. Following capture, his unit was kept in Germany for a few weeks to dismantle a factory for the Russians. Once that task was completed, the prisoners were put into railroad freight cars and transported for eight horrible days through upper Silesia. The men were not allowed to leave the cars once and were given only one cup of wheat to eat each day. Their destination: a labor camp in Jaworzno near Kattowitz in Poland, about four miles from Auschwitz.

In Jaworzno, the prisoners were forced to work in a coal mine under Polish supervision. Receiving only minimal food rations, the men worked ten hours a day. If a prisoner stopped for only a moment to relax, a Polish guard would beat him until he returned to work. The strain began reaping its grim harvest. Having exhausted every ounce of their strength, at the end of their shift many men would sit down in the mine car, fall asleep, and die. More than one-third of the one thousand SS prisoners died in the first few months, so prisoners from the general army, the *Wehrmacht*, were shipped in to replace them.

Reinhold hung weakly to his long-nurtured faith and managed to survive as, one by one, his comrades collapsed. One prisoner, unable to cope any longer, grabbed a guard's rifle and shot the soldier. Then he turned the gun on himself. To stay alive, Reinhold volunteered to perform extra duties in exchange for a larger food ration. But there was never enough to eat. One day, while he was working near the main entrance of the mine, he noticed some oatmeal

Heinz K___.

and rice in a garbage can. Quickly, he scooped the food into his hands but not before a guard spotted him. The guard threw him to the ground. With several other booted soldiers, he walked over Reinhold, and they did not stop until he was bruised and bloody and could no longer move.

However, there were also friendly guards. Some of them even shared their meager lunches with the prisoners, but they were exceptions. Reinhold often tried to take short rests from his work, risking the beating that would result if he were caught. It was better to rest and be bruised than to die of exhaustion.

The eldest Ziefle son came nearest to despair just before his twenty-first birthday, June 22, 1946. He had been able to hide a small piece of bread and a teaspoon of sugar from his regular rations and extra work. This would be his special birthday menu. But the day before his birthday, another prisoner stole his treasure.

As long as Reinhold's sporadic letters arrived, the Ziefles knew that he was alive and remained hopeful of his eventual return.

The son of the neighbor, Heinz K___, had already returned from the war but was marked by death. His mother, who had scoffed at Maria's trust in an unseen God, remained adamant against religious faith.

As Heinz lay wasting away at the hospital in Neckarsulm, Maria approached the woman about her son. "How is Heinz doing? I have heard that his condition has gotten worse."

"Oh, he hasn't been feeling too good, Frau Ziefle—but don't worry he'll be better soon."

"But he has leukemia; he's terminally ill—"

"Don't be so pessimistic! Heinz is too young to die of a disease like that. He's strong. I'm sure he'll recover."

"I wish I could be so optimistic. I'm concerned, though, that he's not ready to die."

Frau K__ eyed Maria suspiciously. "What do you mean by that?"

"I don't think he's made his peace with God."

The woman's face flushed with anger as she glared at Maria. "Don't you dare brainwash my son with your religion. You and your husband had better keep your Jesus talk away from him!" She stormed away.

Lord, take away her blindness, Maria prayed. *Heinz is losing the life in his body and soul, and she refuses to see the truth.*

In the evening, Maria told the family about her encounter with Frau K___. The prayers of their *Dämmerstündle* that evening were not only for their imprisoned brother but also for the K___ family's hardened hearts. All they could do was hope and pray for a change.

Only a few more weeks passed and Frau K___ came to the Ziefles' house, weeping and shaking. "Frau Ziefle," she moaned, "Heinz is dead." Suddenly, she collapsed on Maria's shoulder, wailing loudly, "Why couldn't I do it? Why couldn't I do it?"

Maria led the distraught woman to the sofa and sat down next to her, holding her as she wept. "Tell me—what couldn't you do?" she finally asked when the woman began to quiet down.

Frau K___ could hardly speak. "Heinz was breathing his last, and he said, 'Mother, please pray with me.' I just stood and looked at him; I couldn't do it—not even the Lord's Prayer! Heinz stared at me, and his eyes grew larger and larger, and—and then he died!" She broke again into weeping.

She looked at Maria, her face streaked with tears. "I knelt by my son's bed and told God to take control of my life—that I was sorry for all my rebellion."

Everyone pitches in with reconstruction. Here, bricks are cleaned for reuse.

She looked into Maria's eyes. "Can God take me—after all that I've said against Him?"

Maria smiled. "Dear Frau K___, we have God's promise." She put her arms around the woman and held her tightly. "Let's pray together," she suggested. The two women knelt before the bench of the old pump organ and told God what was on their minds. For Maria, the suffering and humiliation of the last years seemed a small price to pay for this moment. *Lord, if only this had happened before Heinz passed away,* she thought.

But this was not the only fruit of their sufferings. A few months later, as the family ate supper in the light of the glowing wood fire, a knock at the door drew their attention. Georg went to see who it was. He pulled the door open and stared. "Fritz! Come in! Where have you been all these years?"

The baker's former employee followed Georg up into the dining room and began to tell his story. "I was in the Wehrmacht and was captured in Russia. While I was in prison, I had much time to think—and I thought often about this moment." He looked down at the floor and shuffled his feet. "Herr Ziefle—do you still have the Bible I returned to you?" The Ziefles looked at him with surprise. "I have come back to God. I'll never desert Him or my Bible again."

Elated, Georg exclaimed, "Fritz, you have come home in more than one way!" The whole family joined in the rejoicing. When they were seated again and listening to Fritz recount his experiences in Russia, Georg turned to the bookcase and retrieved the Bible that Fritz once had owned. Silently, he handed it to the young man.

Fritz snatched the book and clutched it to his chest. With tears on his face, he whispered, "Lord, forgive me; Your Word and I can never be separated again."

Fritz was dismayed at the news that Reinhold was imprisoned in Poland. He knew how difficult life was in the East. The Ziefles, however, did not allow his comments to cause despair. Instead, they recaptured the happy moments of the past by holding a *Dämmerstündle* again with Fritz.

❧

Postwar reconstruction was now gaining momentum rapidly. Inner turmoil was subsiding as the Poles and other East Europeans had been returned to their countries and as German soldiers came home from Allied prison camps to reestablish their family lives.

The economy, however, was still staggering from the blows of military defeat. Millions of Germans from the eastern half of the country had fled or were expelled to West Germany; population patterns were thus thrown far out of balance. In the slowly recovering economy, jobs for these homeless people were still nonexistent. This created friction between the Germans and the new settlers. The widening rift between the Western Allies and Russia and resulting division of Germany further added to the internal pressure.

In 1948, the Deutsche Mark was instituted to provide a stable currency. Every German citizen was given sixty DM as a start, and old Reichsmarks were exchanged at a rate of 10 RM to 1 DM. With the establishment of the new money system, practically overnight the stores began displaying consumer goods such as bicycles and watches that had been virtually unavailable for years. Even candy was available again.

With the new free market system and the infusion of money through the Marshall Plan, the economic recovery accelerated quickly. Soon, materialism was gaining momentum. The people were frequenting their houses of worship less and less as the siren songs of prosperity and pleasure beckoned more and more loudly.

Georg and Maria and their children were not to be enticed. They had determined their faith in God in earlier times of prosperity; during the years of distress, He proved Himself to them all the more. They had seen the fleeting rewards of men who sought for temporal glory and gratification. They had seen the hate and the cruel pride. And at the end, they had seen the bleak humiliation that comes upon men who live for self. The Ziefles were not rich, but they were deeply satisfied. They still felt the deep anguish of the absence of their firstborn, but they were assured of the eternal joy that was set before them. They would continue in faith.

The few letters from their son continued to be censored heavily. The handwriting looked increasingly unsteady. This fact was cause for concern, and they always directed their anxieties to the One who understood the situation in its entirety.

&ℭ

It was now 1950. Almost five years had passed since Reinhold's capture. One day, Maria casually reached into the brown mailbox and retrieved its contents: one envelope from the German government. Curious, she tore it open and removed the letter. The notice was brief; Reinhold would arrive in Heilbronn by train from Heidelberg in about a week.

Quivering with excitement, Maria wept as she stood outside her house. She could hardly wait for her husband and children to come home so she could

Welcome Home, Reinhold—Upon his return as prisoner of war from 1945 to 1950. The smile on his mother's face and the garland decorating the entrance symbolize the great joy of his homecoming.

tell them the news. The distress of the war had aged her beyond her fifty-two years; now she felt a fresh torrent of vigor within her. Her hopes had not been in vain.

God, protect him for just a few more days. Don't let anything happen to him before he comes home!

The Ziefles prepared frantically for the homecoming. Kurt and Reinhold's room was specially cleaned and decorated. Maria baked and cooked his favorite foods. Ruth made a garland of greenery and spring flowers and hung it over the front door. Helmut, who had just turned eleven, printed a sign that said, "Herzlich Willkommen" (a cordial welcome), and Kurt hung it above the garland. The celebration would be worthy of the chancellor.

❧

The hard wooden bench had no effect as the rhythmic click and sway of the train car lulled Reinhold to sleep. He had tried hard to recall the faces of his parents and siblings, but the five-year ordeal had blurred his memory. As his eyes closed and his head drooped, though, his subconscious replayed razor-sharp images in his mind: Mama's soft eyes, Papa's snappy wit, Kurt's bubbling energy, Ruth's poised consistency, Helmut's curiosity.

A loud voice startled him—the dreaded midnight roll calls still had their effect. Assuring himself that Jaworzno was five hundred miles behind him, he drifted off to sleep again. Normal sleep patterns and a good diet would soon restore his puffy, sallow complexion, but food and rest would not heal a mind scarred by years of constant abuse and humiliation. Even Reinhold's heart, conditioned to love and forgive, was plagued with the whispering taunts of revenge and resentment. The injustice of his ordeal was horribly conspicuous; he had been imprisoned and tortured as a proponent of the very regime he despised. But he was determined not to succumb to such temptation.

&

As the week wore on, the Ziefle family grew jittery with anticipation. Whenever they heard a train whistle sound in the distance, they inwardly braced themselves for the possibility of Reinhold's appearance at their doorstep. They performed faithfully their daily duties, but their minds were virtually fixed on Reinhold's return. Each night, however, they climbed into bed disappointed.

&

It was afternoon as the train moved slowly away from Stuttgart's main station. Reinhold shuffled dejectedly down the aisle toward an empty seat. He slumped into the seat and looked out the window with an aimless stare. His satchel had been stolen. He had left the train to find a gift for Helmut; he would purchase it with the money he had received on his release. When he returned to his seat, the small bag was gone and someone else had taken the obviously unoccupied seat.

The contents of the satchel, though insignificant to most people, were all that Reinhold possessed after his long imprisonment. Although he would be in Heilbronn in less than two hours, he momentarily felt as if he had hardly anything left for which to live. All that remained were the clothes he was wearing. Suddenly, he noticed how pathetic his clothes actually looked in contrast to those

Reinhold can smile again—free at last from the tyranny of man.

of the other passengers. It was humiliating. He did not want to be seen this way on the streets of Sontheim. He would stay at the Heilbronn station until the sun had gone down; then he would walk home. It was Tuesday, April 25.

⁊ℰↄ

Kurt who had been reading a book, stood up to stretch. He walked to the living-room window and looked down. All was quiet. The street always appeared desolate in the twilight. Kurt returned to his chair and resumed reading. The doorbell rang. Kurt casually laid the book aside and approached the stairway. He looked out the window at the head of the stairs. He jumped as if hit by a jolt of electricity.

"Reinhold! It is Reinhold!" he screamed as he ran back to the living room to inform the other family members. "He's here! It's him!"

The others sat for a few moments as if paralyzed. The event for which they had been preparing now seemed to be almost imaginary. Dazed, they rose to their feet and approached the stairway.

Realizing his thoughtlessness, Kurt blurted, "Oh, I must go and unlock the door!" He dashed down the steps.

In a few seconds, Kurt and Reinhold, arm in arm, were ascending the stairs toward their family. Helmut gazed at the brother whom he could barely remember. Reinhold looked closely at the eleven-year-old and exclaimed, "Helmut, you are so big!"

The others stood as if rooted to the spot as Reinhold climbed the steps. Waves of relief and ecstasy poured over them. Finally, Helmut ran to him. The spell was broken. The others surrounded him with their arms as he came to the top of the stairs. They huddled together silently. Somehow Maria was able to have the best position from which to hold him tightly. He bent over and kissed her; the tears on their faces mingled in joy.

Seven years had passed since the family had been parted! Now they were all together—alive. The ecstasy of triumph surged through Maria's soul. She, with her God, had prevailed. The words of Psalm 20:7–8 expressed what she felt.

> Some trust in chariots, and some in horses; but we will remember the name of the Lord our God. They are brought down and fallen; but we are risen, and stand upright.

That all family members kept their faith with the help of the Almighty was a gift of God in view of the influence of National Socialism. Beyond that, Maria considered it a special gift that God kept the entire Ziefle family alive and united them again after the war. She knew that not all brothers and sisters in faith could experience this in the same way. God led others differently.

Epilogue

On October 22, 1956, Georg and Maria Ziefle, with seventeen-year-old Helmut, arrived in the United States as immigrants. Unable at their ages (both were approaching sixty) to acquire a new language, the couple never gained U.S. citizenship. Helmut, however, became a citizen in 1965 at the age of twenty-six. One year later, Georg and Maria returned to their native country and re-settled in Neckarsulm-Amorbach.

Reinhold is married and lives in Neckargartach, a suburb of Heilbronn. He was employed at the NSU factory in Neckarsulm and is now retired. His wife, Margarete (maiden name Wörz), passed away on September 20, 1995.

Kurt emigrated to the United States in 1951 and operated a large dairy farm in upstate New York. He is retired and married to Ruth (maiden name Wirth) from Sontheim.

Ruth was married to Helmut Bauschert and lived in Neckarsulm-Amorbach. She passed away on December 25, 2000, and her husband died on August 15, 1999.

Helmut is married to Christa (maiden name Lembeck) and was a professor of German at Wheaton College, Wheaton, Illinois. He retired in 2001 and has two sons, Helmut and Mark.

Maria Ziefle finally claimed her citizenship in the eternal kingdom on May 17, 1970, at the age of seventy-one and was joined by Georg Ziefle on January 13, 1983, at the age of eighty-two.

They can now see what they had believed by faith.